Simpson Street and Other Plays

Edward Gallardo

Edited by John Antush

Arte Publico Press
Houston, Texas

This volume is made possible through a grant from the Ford Foundation.

Arte Publico Press
University of Houston
Houston, Texas 77204-2090

Gallardo, Edward, 1949 —
　　Simpson Street and Other Plays / Edward Gallardo.
　　ISBN 1-55885-004-X
　　1. Puerto Ricans — New York (N.Y.) — Drama. 2. New York (N. Y.) —
Drama. I. Title.
PS3557.A41175S5　1989
812'.54 — dc20　　　　　　　　　　　　　　89-35415
　　　　　　　　　　　　　　　　　　　　　　　CIP

Cover Photo: Evangelina Vigil-Piñón

Printed in the United States of America

Introduction

Saturday night, February 24, 1979, the second night after the world premiere of Edward Gallardo's play, *Simpson Street*, was no ordinary night of theatre magic at the Puerto Rican Traveling theatre (PRTT) on West 47th Street in New York City. The theatre itself was a far cry from the well-equipped 196-seat theatre and rehearsal space that stands there today after a $3 million renovation. The abandoned and condemned firehouse had not yet been completely outfitted. No permanent seats, no proscenium arch, no curtain; only about 99 folding chairs and a performing platform raised about twelve inches. The set consisted of very realistic furnishings of a Bronx tenement apartment. The first row of folding chairs was less than a foot from the platform. Many people that filed in that evening were well-dressed but not a conventional theatre crowd. There, alongside notable theatre people, city-hall dignitaries, and some critics who had missed the opening were friends and neighbors from the Bronx, cousins from Brooklyn, and others from *El Barrio,* many of whom had never seen a play before. Their unsophisticated behavior betrayed the novelty of the experience. When the house lights went out, the crowd eventually quieted down. When the stage lights came up to begin, they "oohed" and "aahed" and commented noisily on everything. Seeing their friends and neighbors onstage, they became so involved with this true-to-life portrayal of the South Bronx that they found it difficult to distinguish artifice from reality. The actors responded to the vibrations of the audience's rapt attention. At one point in the play when Michael is packing, his mother unexpectedly comes into his room. Michael quickly closes the suitcase and pushes it under the bed; only this time the bedcover does not quite hide it. That night a little grayhaired lady tiptoed around the edge of the platform and onto the stage. Surrepetitiously, but much to the delight of the audience, she covered the suitcase so that Lucy would not discover

3

that her son is leaving home. A theatre of the people and for the people had certainly arrived in New York, and one did not have to be Hispanic to enjoy it.

Although the reviews had been favorable, this was not a critics' crowd. Hispanic audiences in New York do not let the critics dictate their tastes, much less their pleasures. Instead, they tend to trust the word-of-mouth report from neighbors and friends. If the first-nighters put out the word in the community that this is a play to be seen, no critic can kill it. But the critics, the intellectuals, the theatre people, all loved this play. The Hispanic community turned out in force, but other people, many of them non-traditional theatregoers, also found a community of experience in the play. The combined appeal broke all attendance records for the new permanent home of the Puerto Rican Traveling Theatre. This kind of popular success that cut across ethnic, even linguistic, lines established *Simpson Street* as a high point in the movement to return the Hispanic theatre to the people, a movement begun in the sixties and continuing on to the present day.

The golden age of Hispanic theatre came during the twenties and thirties when it was predominantly Spanish and part of the international cultural life of New York City. The Spanish Civil War dissipated some of that cultural impact just as the Puerto Ricans began migrating to New York in large numbers during the forties. The Island did not have a strong theatre tradition among the masses, and theatreowners in New York for some time had regarded straight plays as an elitist art form. The main theatre, El Teatro Hispano, at 116th Street and Fifth Avenue, changed over to showing variety shows and movies to fill the house. Hispanic theatre almost died during the forties and fifties. Nevertheless, the hunger for communal expression was always there. Small groups of actors banded together for single productions and dissolved as funds ran out. One example of this occurred in 1954 when Roberto Rodríguez Suárez presented a new play, *La carreta,* by a little-known Puerto Rican playwright, Réne Márquez, at the Hunts Point Palace in the South Bronx. The story of a *jíbaro* family that migrated from the mountains of Puerto Rico to the slums of San Juan, and finally to the slums of New York City, mirrored in some way the experience of all immigrants. Although the five performances over a single weekend sold out and then some, the money was not enough to support the actors and the theatre. Hundreds of people lined up for tickets the following weekend only to be told there would be no more performances. Interestingly enough, the highly successful English-language production of this same play, *The Oxcart,* in 1966 moved Miriam Colón and others to form the Puerto Rican Traveling Theatre (PRTT) in 1967 so they could bring this play to the people of New York free of charge. Funded largely by Mayor John Lindsay's Summerfare Taskforce, they mounted thirty performances that summer in parks and playgrounds all over New York City. The groundswell became a movement. Other Hispanic theatre companies also enjoyed solid successes. Later, in 1979, *Simpson Street* became a milestone in the movement of Hispanic Theatre out of the ghetto and into the mainstream of American theatre.

The three plays in this collection — *Waltz On A Merry-Go-Round* (1975), *Simpson Street* (1979), and *Women Without Men* (1985) — are all milestones in the development of Hispanic-American drama, but *Simpson Street* represents a watershed. *Simpson Street*'s enormous critical and popular success in New York and Denver as well as in smaller cities like Buffalo, Harrisburg, Hartford, Ithaca, and Springfield, established its place solidly in the mainstream of American drama. Its enthusiastic reception on a seventeen city tour of Spain — including Madrid, Seville, and Valencia — as well as in Puerto Rico, Colombia, and Mexico, made Gallardo one of our internationally acclaimed playwrights. Thus, *Simpson Street* was a breakthrough for Gallardo personally and for New York Puerto Rican playwrights generally. This play called attention to the national significance of the hundreds of other plays growing out of the Hispanic

5

experience in New York and gained for them too, international interest. In the United States, the play speaks with the authentic voice of the Puerto Rican community to all Americans of our deepest longing and fears in all our rich ethnic diversity; abroad, it speaks with the authentic voice of America to all peoples.

Simpson Street also marks the end of the Puerto Rican diaspora. The general mood and feeling of plays written by Puerto Ricans in New York before 1979 was one of exile and of a longing to return "home." The early playwrights tended to see the New York experience as too impersonal, materialistic, and secular to encourage the kind of human relationships that characterize the Island culture. *Simpson Street* is the start of a whole series of plays that speak to that second generation who have no root memories of the Island and who regard New York City as "home." Whereas the earlier plays generally looked back to a happier time and golden land, *Simpson Street* and its successors look forward to sharing in the unfolding history of a larger and more complex world. At the end of the play, Michael's attempt to create his identity as a Puerto Rican in this troublesome environment is the challenge out of which a whole generation of any ethnic origin must make of themselves, in one sense, a new people.

This re-creation of the self is an old and well-known American myth, the American Adam. In the earlier play, *Waltz On A Merry-Go-Round,* the main character, Isabella, takes up the challenge of identity in all the wrong ways. Isabella literally tries to burn her bridges behind her and obliterate all ties with her past. Like Gatsby, she tries to invent an identity that springs from her own "Platonic conception" of herself. In the process she tries to deny her own ethnic origins, her parents, the house she was born and raised in, even her own child. Like Blanche DuBois, Isabella has a dream that hovers somewhere out of sight, a dream of spiritual aspiration. All her misbegotten attempts to realize herself are manifestations of her spirit's resistance to her parents' vulgarity, alcoholism, and cruelty toward Jason, the young man who works for them on their large farm. She cannot quite stoop to her parents' meretricious values, but she has nothing very substantial to put in their place. Her reflex aspirations toward love and justice take the form of sexual favor to the less fortunate boys in her high school. As her sister Sara says, ". . . the poorer the boys, the dirtier, the better." Later Isabella's emotionally complicated affair with Sara's husband, Jason, is on one buried level of her consciousness a spiritual protest against her father's inhuman snobbery. That she herself is afflicted with an air of superiority attests to her own confusion about means and ends. Underneath Isabella's self-centerdness, defensive put-downs, and denial of factual reality is another reality, the reality of the urgings of the spirit toward some heightened awareness, if only she knew what it was and how to achieve it. A bundle of contradictions, Isabella lacks some basic human and social values, but she has a lively spirit that will not settle for less than she can imagine. She does not share in any strong, *jíbaro* culture; she is confined socially to the drifting wreckage of a defeated class, but she does not go down without a fight. Her most positive quality, her vitality, is moving; however, the corruption of her invincible romanticism, with its extreme posturing and all its special complexities, exacts a very high price.

In this developmental sequence the ending of *Waltz* is tragic; the ending of *Simpson Street* is hopeful; but the ending of *Women Without Men* is happy. The most recent of the three plays but set in an earlier time, the 1940's, *Women Without Men* engenders that hopeful but vulnerable sense of life going on as a continuum between past and future. Soledad represents the connecting link between the past which is her mother and the future which is her daughter. Soledad manages in the end to make those necessary discriminations of judgement about what she can choose to reject of the past and what she must necessarily live with. She gains an insight into herself in her daughter's experience and into her mother in her own experience. At the climax, mother and daughter look at each other as if seeing for the first time who they really are. There is a sense of relief, even joy, as they look at each other without the constructions they had created to replace each other. Soledad has asserted her independence as a woman; Orqudea, her mother, is moving out. They share a moment of mutual respect. They are free.

In other ways these three plays constitute a natural group. They form a trio of plays that extend Tennessee William's image of the self trapped within its own skin to the self trapped within its own family. In *Waltz* five sisters vie with each other for redemption from the sins of their parents. Like animals caught in a trap, they writhe in the pain of their own self-destructive behavior. Their common lover and supposed liberator, Jason, turns out to be their predator. *Simpson Street* pits mothers against sons and daughters in an almost Strindbergean struggle for survival. Some escape the family trap; others do not. Those who do always leave something of themselves behind, a good part of themselves. In *Women Without Men* one woman is depressed that her wife-beating husband had been dishonorably discharged from the army and will soon return home. For complicated reasons she cannot leave him. None of these women can escape, but another young woman's, Soledad's, final act of compassion frees her in a more important way. There is a certain heroism in these women for whom flight is not an option, who have to face the rigors of their situation, and who do not cave in.

From the very beginning, Gallardo sets himself to the task of dramatizing the conflict between what people think they want in their conscious will and what in their deepest desires they actually want. Many of Gallardo's characters are caught in a grotesque mode of behavior they neither understand nor wholly approve. The result is that they often do not like themselves very much. No need for masks here, nor even asides, to clarify these personality splits. The divisiveness within the characters themselves is carefully written into the text. In *Waltz* we witness the breakdown of Isabella, the oldest of four sisters in her mid-thirties and her daddy's favorite. High strung, intelligent, fiercely ambitious, Isabella is ashamed of her alcoholic but loving parents, ashamed of her Puerto Rican ancestry, ashamed of her family's modest but respectable life style. She would do anything to get ahead in the world (and she has done some terrible things), but all her attempts to deny her birthright have not gotten her very far. For all her ruthless amorality she has even less to show for it in a material way than the others: "a furnished room in a lousy neighborhood, sharing a bathroom in the hallway with those same people (she) loves to condemn." Some audiences may shrug and say to themselves, "that's the way life is, bad luck"; others may see it as a poetic justice and thank God that they are not the tormented person that Isabella is. But Gallardo does not leave it at that; he never loses firmness of tone about the audiences' complex response to Isabella. For all her quickness of mind and shrewd calculation, we come to understand the defect underlying her bitchiness. Of all the many irreconcilable passions contending within this complicated woman, her love for her sister Sara's husband, Jason, is one of the most entangled. She is attracted to Jason by a curious blend of displaced father love, sibling rivalry, insecurity, many guilts, masochism, and other strands of emotion beyond her control.

In the long first scene of the second act, Isabella tries in vain to make some human contact with others in the living room. She offers to play cards with Henry and Jason, help Sara wash the dishes, talk about poetry with Evelyn, dance with Miriam and Henry. With each overture she grows a little more desperate, and an edginess creeps into her voice. She insults Evelyn, driving her from the room. When Jason will not look up from his newspaper, she taunts him with a humiliating memory from their childhood and threatens to burn his newspaper. In a frenzy of frustration she throws lighted matches at Jason to get his attention. This incident foreshadows the revelation at the climax of the play. All this obnoxious behavior, like an unwilled affliction, only deepens her alienation from her family and hardens Jason's hatred for her. This one scene recapitulates the movement of a lifetime. Isabella compulsively criticizes, insults, taunts when she really wants to help out, cooperate with, and care for her family. She is like a dog who wants to be petted but can only bark. All she can do is humiliate Jason when she really wants him to take her in his arms and dance. We first see the signs of the conflict within Isabella in her erratic behavior. Then we make connections between the surface events that trigger her responses. Gradually we realize the roots of the conflict and with that vision comes a kind of understanding that all ethnic prejudice is a form of self-hatred.

In *Simpson Street* Gallardo again portrays people trapped in one mode of behavior while their deeper longings cry out for another. Rosa Sánchez and her eighteen-year-old daughter Sonia are caught in a cultural, as well as a generational conflict. The cultural *machismo* of Puerto Rico, especially as it has been translated to the mainland, has soured Rosa on marriage and unsettled her sense of her own worth as a woman. Her response to the double strands of *machismo* is to use men sexually the way she perceives men use women. She dresses provocatively and flirts outrageously. She seems to define herself as a woman by her sexual prowess. Not even her best friends' husbands and sons are safe from her voracious sexual appetite. As if her actual conquests are not enough, she boasts of afffairs she never had and complains about propositions she never got. Yet her continual barrage of off-color jokes betrays her intense dislike of sex.

Nowhere in Rosa's conflict within herself more apparent than in her ambivalence toward her daughter. She wants Sonia to go out with boys, get married, and have healthy relationships with men. At the same time her maternal concern makes her want to protect Sonia from men and marriage. Other factors such as fear of aging, sexual rivalry, jealousy of Sonia's youth, fear of being unloved, and more, complicate this mother/daughter relationship. Toward the end of the play these conflicting emotions come to a head when Sonia finally announces that Tony has proposed and she has accepted. Everyone else is genuinely happy for her, congratulating her, giving her advice, celebrating; but

Rosa remains silent. As Sonia starts to leave, she says "Mommy, haven't you got anything to say to me?" (81). After a meaningful emotional pause during which we feel the mother's desire to hug her child and wish her happiness, the cynic in Rosa says, "I think you're a fool." Fighting back the tears, Sonia leaves without her mother's blessing.

Set in 1944, *Women Without Men* explores the problem of women in a male dominated society when the men are away at war. Left on their own the women must set their own standards for proper social and sexual conduct, much to the dismay of their supervisor in the Betty Blouse Factory, Orqudea Juventud. Although Women portrays several variations on these young ladies' response to their new-found freedom, the focus of this play falls on the mother/daughter relationship. Orquídea tries to set a standard of behavior for her young seamstresses, including her own twenty-eight-year-old daughter, Soledad; but her religious fanaticism, racism, and jingoistic patriotism only reflect much of what is wrong with society at large. Although married and with an twelve-year-old daughter of her own, Soledad still lives under her mother's domination. When her husband Armando went into the army, he invited his mother-in-law to move into his house and care for his wife and daughter. A physically and emotionally abusive mother, Orquídea confuses her love for her child with her own self-loathing. Soledad, of course, perceives her mother's viciousness toward her as hatred, and deep down she believes she must be evil to deserve such cruel punishment. Toward the end of Act II the uncomprehending Soledad exclaims, "God damn you, Mamá, all I ever wanted from you was love, but all you ever gave me was the Ten Commandments bashed into my skull."

Soledad determines that at least her daughter Evelyn will not grow up unloved, swearing to Carlotta, "I can't let her grow up like I did. She's gonna know that somebody loves her, no matter what." But Carlotta recalls that she had a mother like that, until her mother found out her little girl had lesbian tendencies.

Carlotta ruefully says that sometimes she wishes her mother had never loved her at all. The remark triggers Soledad's memory of an incident that happened the day before while Soledad visited her daughter away at summer camp. Soledad had eagerly anticipated that visit, but she forgot to bring some dresses she had promised her little girl. Evelyn started complaining that her mother did not love her and that she herself loved only her daddy. "I didn't even realize I had begun hitting her," Soledad confesses. "Hitting her with such a vengeance I was my mother all over again with her crying out for her daddy the way that I used to cry out for mine." In a flash Soledad recognizes how precariously close love is to hate. Later, at the moment of truth in this play, this understanding provides a contructive link in Soledad's future relations with both her mother and her daughter.

Gallardo's plays have the strength of being rooted in the actual, but each play makes a gesture toward a larger world of meaning. *Waltz* is not merely a detective story. It has suspense, foreshadowing, irony, and a very theatrical surprise ending; however, the play's significance goes beyond mere melodrama. The throwing of the lighted matches has some of the dark foreboding of the place where three roads meet and of that other woman who tried to circumvent Fate by giving her baby son to a kindly shepherd to kill. The play's meaning goes beyond any special "message" of the wages of Isabella's sin. The play leaves us with a strong image of home, where self-definition starts, and of how the forging of the self cannot be achieved by denying one's birthright. By the same token, *Simpson Street,* in juxtaposing the crucial decisions of Michael and Angela to leave and not to leave home, has a quality beyond psychology, an aesthetic appeal that teases the mind. Apart from what the play may teach us about how to order our lives, an incommensurable element remains. The image of the brother and sister working out their perfectly logical choices gives the play a powerful stage effect over and above any intellectual message. And in *Women* the final image of Orquídea and Soledad looking at each other as if for the first time haunts the mind like the choosing of the right casket at Belmont whereby we may learn not to choose by the false constructions we create to replace each other. Gallardo's plays are held together by a dominant image given consistent embodiment in the structural relationships of events and characters. They speak to us all about some of our deepest inner conflicts. These plays go a long way toward making the theatre an integral part of our society and not just an appendage to it.

John V. Antush
Fordham University

Simpson Street

by

Edward Gallardo

Dedicated to Yolanda Gallardo,
without whom I would not be a writer.

And to Joan Gallardo and Dorothy Roggio
for always being there.

Characters:

LUCY RODRIGUEZ: An overweight but attractive woman in her forties. She is Angela's and Michael's mother.

ANGELA: A striking young woman born in New York. She is Lucy's daughter in her late twenties.

ELVA CRUZ: A short woman in her forties but with a bosom that would be envied by an Amazon queen, an alcoholic.

ROSA SANCHEZ: A woman in her mid-forties but who believes she is twenty and dresses accordingly.

MICHAEL RODRIGUEZ: A young man in his early twenties. Though he has a strong presence, he has not totally lost the look of a frightened child.

SONIA SANCHEZ: An attractive, energetic girl of eighteen. She is Rosa's daughter and seems to take life as it comes.

ACT ONE

SCENE ONE

The setting is of the Rodríguez apartment. Visible are the kitchen, the living room and MICHAEL'*s room. It is a clean, but poorly-furnished apartment located on Simpson Street, a street in a run-down area of the Bronx. As the lights come up Spanish music can be heard coming from the phonograph in the living room. It is a quiet romantic record. All of the women are drinking, but it is apparent that* ELVA *has been affected the most.* ANGELA *is having a beer. They're all preparing for* MICHAEL'*s homecoming party.*

LUCY: What time is it?

ROSA: Five minutes after you last asked.

ANGELA: It's a little after three, Ma.

LUCY: Ay, Michael should be here soon.

ROSA: Yeah. Sonia called right before they left.

LUCY: That was so nice of your kid to go and pick him up. . .
Angela, is the door locked?

ANGELA: I think so.

LUCY: Go and check it. I don't want to spoil the surprise.
(ANGELA *checks the front door in the living room.*)

ROSA: *Mira*, calm down. You're making me nervous.

LUCY: I'm just so happy.

ANGELA: It's locked.

LUCY: I can't believe he's finally coming home.

ROSA: How long's he been gone now?

LUCY: A year. God, I get sick every time I think about it.

ROSA: I just hope he hasn't changed too much.

ANGELA: He most likely has.

LUCY: Angela, don't say that. Your brother is gonna be the
same.

ANGELA: For his sake I hope not. (*The record finishes.*)

LUCY: *Ay*, I love that record.

ROSA: Yeah.

ELVA: (*Who has begun to cry.*) I hate it! I hate it!

ANGELA: (*To* ELVA.) Hey, what's the matter with you?

LUCY: *Oye, nena, ¿qué te pasa?*

ROSA: Ah, leave her alone. If she wants to cry, let her. (ELVA's *sobbing becomes louder.*)

ANGELA: Oh, my God.

LUCY: Come on Elva, you're wetting all the cold cuts. (*They all burst into laughter as* ELVA *slips forward and almost appears to be resting her breasts on the table.*)

ROSA: *Coño*, take your tits out of the cheese!

ELVA: That song reminds me of Bosco!

LUCY: Bosco?

ANGELA: Who the hell was Bosco? (LUCY *and* ROSA *laugh loudly.*)

ELVA: Shut up!

ROSA: Oh, stop being such a *pendeja* already.

ELVA: (*Turning on her instantly.*) Don't you tell me what to do.

ROSA: Eh, eh . . . *cuidado* . . . *suavecito* . . . take it slow lady . . . don't push.

ELVA: (*Standing over her, her breasts almost touching* ROSA's *face.*) Don't tell me . . .

ROSA: Eh, eh . . . ay, take them things out of my face.

LUCY: Come on, Elva, don't spoil everything.

ELVA: You're both just jealous of me, that's all. (*To* ANGELA.) They're both jealous because of me and Bosco.

ROSA: *Ay, coño!* (ROSA *and* LUCY *laugh.*) Fool! Imagine us being jealous because of Bosco.

ELVA: I know. You think I don't know but I know.

LUCY: You don't know anything.

ANGELA: Calm down Elva.

ELVA: Angela, they both tried to take him away from me.

LUCY: *Ay, m'ija*, that hard up I've never been.

ROSA: And what would I want with him?

LUCY: You know.

ROSA: Oh! To do *cositas* with, huh Elva? (*As she says this she makes an obscene hand gesture towards her. She and* LUCY *continue laughing*.) Ah, what are you worried about anyway. You're with Carlos now. You shouldn't even be thinking about Bosco.

ELVA: You were always trying to take him away from me.

ROSA: Believe me, if I would have tried I would have succeeded.

ELVA: (*She is on top of* ROSA *again*.) No woman can take a man away from me.

ROSA: *Ay*, shut up before you make me mad. And get them things away from me, I've told you already. If I see them watermelons again I'm gonna cut 'em off and give them to Michael as dessert!

LUCY: How come you always gotta get like this? How come you always gotta start a scene?

ELVA: I didn't do nothing.

LUCY: Damn it, you shouldn't drink so much. Even today, with Michael coming home. Well, let me tell you, you just better not start fighting in front of him.

ELVA: I'm not doing nothing. It's her . . .

ROSA: Me?

LUCY: No, no, you're fine Elva.

ELVA: I am. And I didn't drink hardly nothing.

ROSA: Then how come you're the only one who's drunk?

ELVA: I am not drunk!

ROSA: You drank almost the whole damn bottle. Thank God we bought two.

ELVA: Liar!

ROSA: *Que ya*; I've warned you. Don't start. Don't spoil Lucy's day for her.

ELVA: But what am I doing? Am I bothering you Lucy? Huh, am I?

LUCY: *Mira*, Elva, just control yourself. And finish making that platter before all the cold cuts dry up. (ELVA *continues to cut up pieces of cheese; however, she continually eats them herself.*)

ROSA: Speaking of cold cuts, when I went to get them for you this morning that old *peo* Irving, the butcher, made a pass at me.

LUCY: You gotta be kidding.

ROSA: No, I swear on my mother. (*She blesses herself.*) This morning when I go in he tells me that if I go in the back with him he'll give me a free pound of ground beef.

ELVA: You went, right?

ROSA: *M'ija*, I may not be Marilyn Monroe but I'm sure as hell better than a hamburger. Now if he had said sirloin steak or filet mignon I might have thought about it.

LUCY: Well, what did you tell him?

ROSA: I feel bad now. I almost gave him a heart attack, the old guy. I told him if I went in the back with him . . . (*Gesturing.*) I was gonna take his kosher salami there and shove it through the meat grinder.

LUCY: *Ay* Rosa you're so fresh.

ROSA: Me? Me? That old bastard would deserve it. They think 'cause a woman ain't got no husband living with her that she'll go with anybody, no matter who they are.

ELVA: You must have done something to encourage him.

ROSA: What are you saying now?

ELVA: That you must have encouraged him. He never made a pass at me.

ROSA: Elva, Rin Tin Tin wouldn't make a pass at you . . . unless it was to lift his leg!

ELVA: Hey Rosa . . .

ROSA: Oh I'm only joking.

LUCY: *Mira* you two, enough. Angela, did you get the cake?

ANGELA: How many times are you gonna ask me that?

LUCY: Oh, that's right.

ROSA: What kind did you get?

ANGELA: A chocolate layer.

ROSA: Oooh, I love chocolate layers. Lemme see. (LUCY *takes the cake from the refrigerator.*)

LUCY: I should have gotten it myself. I told her to go to the Valencia Bakery and get one, but instead she comes in with this stupid chocolate cake from the A & P downstairs.

ANGELA: I didn't have time to be going to Valencia's for no cake.

LUCY: *Bueno*, then you could have at least gotten one from the bakery around the corner.

ANGELA: I told you I tried.

ROSA: Don't worry Lucy, this one's fine.

LUCY: Maybe with a candle on it it'll look better. (*She places a candle in the center of the cake.*) No help.

ROSA: It's fine.

LUCY: It's just that I wanted a nice fancy one.

ANGELA: Well, all the nice fancy ones either said happy birthday or had a bride and groom stuck on top of them. Anyway, the cakes in that place taste terrible. I think they use lard instead of butter.

LUCY: *Ay* Angela . . .

ANGELA: It's true. And I don't even wanna think about what they use for whipped cream.

LUCY: Don't make me nauseous.

ROSA: (*Seeing* ELVA *eating the cheese.*) *Oye tú*, she said make the platter, she didn't say eat it.

ELVA: I'm hungry.

ROSA: *Mira*, there's gonna be nothing left for when Michael gets here.

LUCY: (*Looking around the living room.*) The house looks okay?

ROSA: It looks beautiful.

LUCY: You like the decorations?

ROSA: *Sí m'ija*, they look fabulous.

ANGELA: You'd swear this was a birthday party or something.

LUCY: Well, it is a special day.

ANGELA: I'm just surprised that you didn't buy everybody party hats and put up a piñata or a pin the tail on the donkey.

ROSA: She was going to, but I figured we could use Elva instead. Bigger target.

ELVA: Oh, shut up.

LUCY: You should have seen me, Rosa, standing on a chair trying to put up the balloons. I looked like a whale out of water.

ROSA: Why didn't you wait for me to help?

LUCY: You've helped me more than enough . . . with the shopping and cleaning and all.

ROSA: *Ay*, the rice! (*She runs to the stove and looks in a pot. She turns off the gas and tastes the rice.*)

LUCY: *¿Se quemó?*

ROSA: *¡Perfecto!* Another triumph.

LUCY: Good. I want everything to be just right.

ANGELA: Don't worry so much Ma, everything's gonna be fine.

LUCY: I hope. I even made a *promesa* to *La Caridad* that I'd light a candle for a month.

ROSA: That's gonna be a pretty big candle.

LUCY: *No seas bruta.* A different candle everyday.

ROSA: *Ay m'ija*, don't you ever get tired of praying?

LUCY: Ay, Rosa, you shouldn't joke like that.

ROSA: Who's joking? The only thing I ever pray for is for my husband to drop dead so I can collect his insurance money.

LUCY: Don't talk like that.

ROSA: Why not?

LUCY: He's not that bad.

ROSA: (*Raising middle finger.*) *Esto* he's not. Okay, *quizás ahora* that he's getting old, he's better. But that still doesn't change what that bastard put me through when we were together.

LUCY: You weren't exactly a saint either.

ROSA: That's true, but that bastard is the devil himself.

(ANGELA *takes another beer from the refrigerator*.) Don't
you want a real drink?

ANGELA: No, I've got a headache. Headache, my ass, a hang-
over.

ROSA: You go out last night?

ANGELA: Yeah.

ROSA: I didn't see you.

ANGELA: I had a date.

ROSA: Anyone I know?

ANGELA: I didn't ask.

LUCY: Why don't you take some aspirin or something?

ANGELA: I've already taken four today. What I could really
use is more sleep.

LUCY: Go lie down. I'll wake you up when Michael comes.

ANGELA: No, I tried that this morning and when I fell back
asleep I had this terrible nightmare. I dreamt I was pregnant.

LUCY: What's so bad about that?

ANGELA: Nothing, except that I was still married to Nandy.
And we were living in this white cardboard box that had no
doors and no windows. We just sat there and stared at each
other. Then I had the baby and Fernando had on this big,
stupid smile all through my labor. And the baby, instead of
crying, had the same stupid smile.

ROSA: Oooh, that sounds horrible.

LUCY: Speaking of Fernando, he called before.

ANGELA: Again? Well, what did you tell him?

LUCY: That you were out shopping.

ANGELA: You should have said I dropped dead. (ELVA *makes
herself another drink*.)

LUCY: *Oye*, leave something for the rest of us.

ELVA: I'm going to the bathroom, Lucy. I'll be right back. (*She
exits*.)

ROSA: What happened between you two? I thought you were
so happy.

ANGELA: Nothing happened. That's the whole problem. In

four years of marriage, nothing happened.

LUCY: He loves you, Angela.

ANGELA: So what?

ROSA: What the hell is love anyway. It's over in five minutes like everything else.

LUCY: He said he had to talk to you. That he'd call back.

ANGELA: Did you tell him not to bother?

LUCY: How could I say that? He's your husband.

ROSA: She's right, Lucy. Good for you, Angela. Good for you.

LUCY: Rosa, please . . .

ROSA: No, I know what she means . . .

LUCY: *Mira*, I'm talking to my daughter. *No te metas*, okay?

ROSA: (*Feigning being offended.*) Excuse me . . .

ANGELA: Ma, I've already wasted four years of my life.

LUCY: Marriage isn't wasting your life.

ANGELA: It sure as hell is when you're expected to sit home and do nothing except wait for your husband to come home. Well, I am through with waiting and I'm through with Nandy and I am through with all this marriage shit. Damn, I don't wanna talk to him when he calls. I don't even wanna be here.

LUCY: You can't go out. What about Michael?

ANGELA: Don't worry Ma, I'll be here to say hello to Michael.

LUCY: Okay, but don't mention nothing to him about your problems with Fernando, alright?

ANGELA: *Ay* Ma! Damn, I don't believe that man. I walked out of there a week ago yesterday and he's called me how many times a day since?

LUCY: Maybe something's wrong.

ANGELA: Oh, something's wrong all right. His pride is hurt. His machismo's damaged.

LUCY: Talk to him, Angela. See what he wants.

ANGELA: Ma, you can't talk to him because he never listens. Never. The same way he never wants anything, he demands things. I know if I talk to him he's gonna demand that I go

back to him, and I'm sorry, Ma, I am much too young to be
so bored. Shit, he's even gotta bore me in my dreams.

LUCY: Angela, maybe your leaving has made him think ... has
made him change.

ROSA: Men never change.

LUCY: Rosa ... I'm telling you for your own good. You don't
know what it's like to be alone.

ANGELA: What makes you such an authority on loneliness?
Because Daddy left? Well the man I married might just as
well have been gone. I know what it's like being alone, Ma.
That's why I left him. I don't wanna end up like you.

LUCY: My life isn't exactly over. I've still got you kids ...

ANGELA: Well, I want more than that. I don't want to be forty
years old and not even have memories. I don't wanna live
through my kids because I never had a life of my own.

LUCY: Angela, you've lived with the man for four years. Don't
you feel you at least owe him a chance to talk?

ANGELA: The only one I feel I owe anything is to myself.
(ELVA *re-enters*.)

ROSA: Hey come on, snap out this mood, the both of you. Why
don't we all go out tonight? Let's go to La Campana or
someplace.

LUCY: No Rosa, I'm really not up to any of that.

ROSA: Oh, come on. Michael would enjoy it. He can see his old
friends again.

LUCY: Well, he can see them without me.

ROSA: Roberto's even talked about giving him his old job back.

LUCY: Good for him. Now can we please change the subject?
You know how I feel about that place.

ROSA: That's right I know. You used to love it.

LUCY: Used to and now are two different times.

ROSA: Roberto's been asking a lot about you, too.

LUCY: (*Attempting non-chalance.*) Oh, yeah?

ROSA: I got the feeling he wants to get back together with you.

LUCY: *Ay para con eso ya.*

ROSA: It's true. He told me he still loves you.

LUCY: Well I don't feel nothing for him.

ROSA: Then how come you're blushing. Look at her, Angela, she's turning red as a tomato.

LUCY: I'm not blushing. It's just my high blood pressure.

ROSA: My ass it is. You know you still love him.

LUCY: Do I?

ROSA: You're damned right you do. That's why you don't go no place anymore. Why you haven't even looked at another man since he left you.

LUCY: He didn't leave me, I threw him out. And please don't mention anything to Michael about Roberto.

ROSA: What are you talking about. He likes him.

LUCY: That's what I thought too.

ELVA: Yeah, I don't wanna go there either. Carlos doesn't even like me spending so much time here without him. If he saw me at La Campana he'd kill me.

ROSA: If my husband tried to lay a hand on me again I'd cut his balls off and that bastard knows it. I've got him like a trained dog now. Men need that.

ANGELA: I'm beginning to think so.

ELVA: Yeah, but Carlos . . .

ROSA: Oh, fuck Carlos. And in his uniform I wish I could.

ELVA: Rosa . . .

ROSA: Oh, don't start getting jealous again. I ain't interested in Carlos. To me he's nothing more than a bastard cop.

LUCY: Enough Rosa.

ROSA: No, I'm sorry, but it's the truth. I can't stand that man. He always walks around with that look on his face like he's smelling shit. Though living with Elva he probably is.

ELVA: Hey, what you mean . . .

ROSA: Oh, sit down. (*There is a knock on the door.*)

LUCY: *Ay Dios mío*, it's Michael. (*Calling to the door.*) Just a minute. *Ay* Angela, where's the sign?

ANGELA: (*Taking a rolled up sign from the corner.*) It's right here, Ma.

LUCY: Okay. Stand in the living room. Rosa you take the other side. (*She does. The sign reads "Welcome Home Michael."* LUCY *places* ELVA *next to them.*) Here, you hold the cake. (*Calling the door.*) I'll be right there. Is everybody ready?

ROSA: Yes, just hurry up! (LUCY *opens the door and* MICHAEL RODRIGUEZ *and* SONIA SANCHEZ *enter, each carring a suitcase.*)

LUCY: Michael! (*She hugs him. All the rest begin to sing.*)

ALL: For he's a jolly good fellow
   For he's a jolly good fellow
   For he's a jolly good fellow
   Which nobody can deny! (*They all greet him loudly with the exception of* ELVA *who passes out, falling on the cake.*)

LUCY: ¡Coño! (*Everyone but* LUCY *laughs.*) Ay, Michael, your cake!

MICHAEL: The hell with the cake, Ma. Is she all right?

SONIA: Should I wake her up, Ma?

ROSA: Nah, leave her there. At least she's quiet.

LUCY: She had to spoil everything.

ANGELA: (*Hugging* MICHAEL.) Wow, you look terrific!

MICHAEL: Yeah, sure.

ANGELA: You do. (SONIA, *who has been trying to awaken* ELVA *finally succeeds. However, she wakes up grumbling and fighting.*)

ELVA: What's going on? What's happening? What's the matter? (*In her fighting she has pushed* SONIA *so that she falls. Everyone is laughing.*)

LUCY: You just passed out, *pendeja*, that's what's the matter.

ELVA: I did not!

ANGELA: I'd better clean up this mess.

ELVA: Where'd this cake come from? Who threw this cake at me? (*Sees* ROSA.) You did it! You did it!

ANGELA: Sonia please, before I kill her, take her into my room.

ELVA: I haven't finished my drink.

LUCY: No, but your drink has finished you.

ELVA: I wanna go home.

LUCY: *Mira*, nobody leaves my house in that condition. Now just stop being a pain and go inside. (SONIA *leads her off. She is mumbling something to herself.*)

ROSA: ¡*Qué loca, coño*!

LUCY: She had to go and ruin everything.

MICHAEL: Are you kidding! I never got such a greeting in my life!

LUCY: But your cake. *Ay bendito.* When she sobers up I'm gonna kill her. No two ways about it. Today she dies. I wanted everything to be just right.

MICHAEL: Everything's perfect. Besides, I don't think I would have recognized Elva standing up.

LUCY: (*Hugging him.*) I'm just so happy you're finally home. I don't want nothing to spoil it. I don't want no one to upset you.

ANGELA: Hey, it's really great to see you!

MICHAEL: Thanks, it's great to be home. The house looks wonderful, Ma.

LUCY: Thank you.

ROSA: She decorated it all by herself.

MICHAEL: It's really terrific.

ROSA: (*After a pause.*) Well, anybody for a drink?

MICHAEL: I would love one.

LUCY: Can you? You know, with the medication and everything. . .

MICHAEL: I didn't take any today.

LUCY: *Ay* Michael, that's not good.

MICHAEL: Don't worry, Ma. The doctor said it would be okay.

LUCY: Doctors, what do they know? (*They all go into the kitchen.* MICHAEL *sees the platters on the table.*)

MICHAEL: Wow, just look at all of that.

ROSA: You should have seen it before Elva got to it. She ate more than half.

LUCY: I won't forgive her for this. She's never coming back into this house. (ROSA *and everybody drink.*)

MICHAEL: Relax, Ma.

LUCY: I wish I could. My nerves are forget it today.

MICHAEL: Want a tranquilizer? I've got plenty in my suitcase.

LUCY: Ay Michael, don't talk like that. . . . I can't believe my son's finally home. . . . Well, Michael how are you? How do you feel?

MICHAEL: Fine. Never better.

SONIA: (*Offstage.*) Damn it, cut it out and get to bed already!

LUCY: She shouldn't drink if she's gonna get like that.

SONIA: (*Offstage.*) Oh shit!

LUCY: Hey, what's going on in there?

SONIA: (*Offstage.*) You wouldn't believe . . . (*Enters.*) She just threw up all over the place. Damn! Where's the mop, Lucy?

LUCY: No, *m'ija*, don't do that. I'll get it.

SONIA: Nah, it's okay.

LUCY: It's over by the sink. (SONIA *gets it.*)

MICHAEL: Let me help you.

SONIA: You just stay where you are. Be back in a minute. *Fo!* (*Exits into room.*)

LUCY: Throwing up all over my house! *Dios mío*, what else is gonna happen to me?

ANGELA: What are you talking about? It's my room she threw up in.

ROSA: Well Michael, tell me all about it.

ANGELA: Rosa, what the hell kind of question is that? He wasn't on vacation you know.

MICHAEL: It's okay, Angela, I don't mind.

ROSA: Sorry if I said something stupid. *Coño, en esta jodía casa no se puede hablar.*

MICHAEL: Hey look, will everybody relax already? You know, in a way it was kind of like a vacation.

LUCY: *Ay, Miguel, no digas eso.*

MICHAEL: It's true. It's not like what you think. It wasn't like there were bars on the windows and locks on everything, you know. It really was nice. And in a way I even think I'm gonna miss it.

LUCY: Don't talk like that. I don't want to hear any more about it. . . . I missed you so much. And you look so damned good. I don't remember you ever looking better.

MICHAEL: Thanks. Well, how has everything been here?

ANGELA: Fine, wonderful. Ma's working as a topless waitress, I'm hooking and Rosa there's still giving it away for free.

LUCY: Angela, don't say that. He might believe you.

ANGELA: Nah, everything's the same as when you left.

MICHAEL: Does anything ever change around here?

ANGELA: You're telling me.

MICHAEL: How's Nandy?

ANGELA: That's a long story.

LUCY: *Mira*, he doesn't wanna hear about your problems right now.

ANGELA: I know, Ma. I'm not saying nothing.

MICHAEL: Hey, is something wrong?

LUCY: No, nothing. Nothing.

ANGELA: I'll tell you about it later.

MICHAEL: You gonna be around for a while?

ANGELA: You ain't getting rid of me that easy.

MICHAEL: You know, I really missed you. I really missed all of you.

ROSA: Before I forget, Michael, Roberto said to say hello.

MICHAEL: Thanks.

LUCY: *Coño*, is everybody deaf? Everything I said not to talk about you're talking about.

MICHAEL: It's okay, Ma. Just relax.

LUCY: I just don't want nothing to bother you. Ay, Michael, I'm so sorry that all of this had to happen. I'm sorry that you had to go into that hospital in the first place.

MICHAEL: Ma, I was really able to think things out there. And that's what I needed to do more than anything, to think things out for myself. I'm not ashamed about what happened Ma, and you shouldn't be either. I had to grow up. It's as simple as that. And that hospital helped me to do it. Try to understand that.

SONIA: (*Re-entering.*) Damn, no sooner do I get her back into bed, she starts calling me Bosco and tries to pull me into bed with her.

ANGELA: Now that Elva's not here, will somebody please tell me, who the hell was this guy Bosco?

LUCY: *Ay Dios*, Bosco goes back about twenty years. He was this *dominicano* she went out with. And if you think Carlos is horrible, he looks like Rudolf Valentino next to Bosco.

ROSA: (*Laughing.*) Remember what he looked like?

LUCY: (*Laughing also.*) Do I. Damn was he ugly. He was real skinny and had a thick moustache . . .

ROSA: Yeah, it always looked like he had a cunt pasted on his upper lip.

ANGELA: Oh, my God.

ROSA: And remember how short he was? He was a runt. Everytime I talked to him I kept hitting him in the eye with my tit.

ANGELA: That's probably why he left her. Too many headaches from being banged on the head so much.

ROSA: Especially with her *montañas*.

ANGELA: What did she see in him anyway?

ROSA: (*Extending her arms.*) He probably had one this big.

LUCY: Ay, Rosa!

ROSA: Bueno, if her *tetas* are any indication of the rest of her, she'd need one that big.

LUCY: Don't be such a pig!

SONIA: Yeah, how come you always gotta be so filthy?

ROSA: You shut up. (*To* LUCY.) And you, just remember I knew you before you became a saint.

ANGELA: Whatever happened to him?

ROSA: To Bosco? He just left one day, that's all. He told her he had to go back to Santo Domingo to settle some affairs and she never heard from him again.

ANGELA: Maybe something happened to him over there.

ROSA: Yeah, the same thing that happens to every man you believe in. He marries somebody else. Remember, Lucy?

LUCY: *Ay, sí, pobre* Elva, she never got over him.

ROSA: He settled his affairs all right. A couple of months later she even went down there looking for him. What she found was that he already had a wife. I mean Elva's a pain in the ass, but nobody deserves that.

SONIA: (*Teasing.*) I don't know . . .

ROSA: That's right, you don't know. You don't know nothing. Especially about men.

SONIA: Are you kidding? With you as my teacher?

ROSA: Michael, this *idiota*, a guy even looks at her and she runs.

SONIA: That's because you're always pushing me out of the way to get to him first . . . And anyway, you don't know what I do when I'm out alone.

ROSA: You do the same thing when you're alone as when we're together. Nothing. *Nada. Caca.* That's what you do. Sometimes I swear you must be Elva's daughter and not mine. You're even getting to look like her.

SONIA: Oh, please . . .

ROSA: I swear, Michael, she's really good for nothing. She's been out of school for over a month now and she can't even find a job.

SONIA: I can get a job any time I want. I'm just waiting for you to die so I can take over your corner.

ROSA: Don't hold your breath. Even dead I'd be better sex than you.

LUCY: *Oye*, it's not nice for a mother and daughter to talk to each other like that.

ROSA: *Ay*, I forgot Virgin Lucy was here. (*She and* LUCY *smile at each other indicating* SONIA.) *Sí, pero ésta, bueno* you know how I feel about marriage, I wouldn't wish it on my worst enemy, but this one is such a pain sometimes that I wish she'd hurry up and find somebody and get married. I think that's the only way I'll ever stop supporting her.

SONIA: You believe this?

ANGELA: *Ay* leave her alone. What the hell's she need to get married for?

SONIA: That's right. I'll get married when I'm ready. And that just might be sooner than you think.

MICHAEL: Is there something going on I don't know about?

SONIA: Maybe.

LUCY: How mysterious . . .

ROSA: Who you gonna marry? That guy Tony you've been writing to?

SONIA: Could be.

LUCY: Could be . . . Maybe . . . Our Lady of the Secrets here.

ROSA: *Ay m'ija*, you'd have to be crazy. You come from two different worlds.

SONIA: That might not be so bad.

ANGELA: Yeah, that's what I thought when I married Nandy.

ROSA: And even you two have more in common.

SONIA: How do you know? You've never even met him.

ROSA: I just know, that's how. You've shown me pictures of the college man, and I've seen his letters . . .

SONIA: You read my letters?

ROSA: Well, then you shouldn't leave them around, you know how I am. You should see, Lucy, he looks about as Latin as Boy George.

SONIA: Well, you're the one who always told me to marry somebody a little lighter.

ROSA: A little lighter, yes, but I didn't say to get ridiculous either. I didn't tell you to marry the Pillsbury Doughboy!

MICHAEL: Sonia, you really serious about getting married?

SONIA: Who isn't?

LUCY: My kids for one.

MICHAEL: Ma, I just got back. Don't start with the marrying

again. I will get married in my own good time.

LUCY: Yes, but I would like to see my grandchildren before I'm nine hundred.

ANGELA: Maybe I'll stop taking the pill.

LUCY: I said grandchildren, not little bastards.

ANGELA: A child is a child, Ma.

LUCY: And a bastard is a bastard! *Ay*, Michael, you see how she is? She says things like that just to bother me.

MICHAEL: She's only kidding, Ma.

LUCY: Sometimes I wonder.

ANGELA: Well, you can stop your wondering and worrying. There's no way I'm bringing a kid into this world.

LUCY: And if I had felt that way, where would you two be?

MICHAEL: Probably a lot happier.

LUCY: *Ay*, Michael, don't say that.

MICHAEL: I'm sorry, Ma. I didn't mean it.

ANGELA: Not me. Sometimes I feel like getting a hysterectomy just so I don't have to worry no more.

LUCY: Enough Angela. That's not how I brought you up.

ROSA: *Ay*, leave them alone. They're not kids anymore. You've done what you could for them, now your job is over.

LUCY: Because they're grown up doesn't mean nothing. You're a mother, Rosa, how can you tell me you don't care what happens to your daughter? That your job is over?

SONIA: Are you kidding? She's been on unemployment since I was three.

ROSA: *Y tú cállate*, or I'm gonna put my hand to work on your face.

LUCY: *Ay*, the world has just changed too much for me. Before people used to be proud to be married, to have children. I'll never forget how happy I was the day I got married . . . Wait a minute . . . (*She exits hurriedly.*)

ROSA: Where are you going?

ANGELA: Ma, don't take that out now.

ROSA: Watch. The same as always.

LUCY: (*Carrying a wedding gown.*) Look. I still have it after all these years.

SONIA: It's beautiful, Lucy.

LUCY: Isn't it? It's all hand-made. God, I don't believe I ever fit in it.

ROSA: I don't believe you ever wore white.

LUCY: *Mira fresca*, I was a virgin when I got married.

ROSA: Don't blame me for it.

ANGELA: Ma, will you put the dress away?

LUCY: You know, Sonia, with a hem it might fit you. You could borrow it for your wedding if you want.

SONIA: You mean it? Well, if I get married I'll take you up on it.

LUCY: I was saving it for my daughter, but . . .

ANGELA: Here we go again.

LUCY: This one gets married in City Hall. Can you believe that? City Hall! And this one, your guess is as good as mine when he'll get married.

MICHAEL: I'll get married, Ma. I'll get married.

ROSA: You know damned well you would die if he got married. You know you don't want no woman taking your baby away from you.

LUCY: Oh, shut up, I do so want him to get married.

ANGELA: Yeah, and I'll go back to Nandy and we can get married again.

LUCY: Maybe if you had gotten married in church the first time you would have been happier.

ANGELA: Okay Ma. Michael and I will both get married in church. We'll have a double ceremony and that way we can both have as happy a life as you.

LUCY: My life was happy. Your father and I did have a happy life together.

ANGELA: Yeah, you were so happy that's why you used to fight all the time. That's why he left.

LUCY: Angela, that's not true.

ANGELA: You forget I wasn't that young when that happened.

LUCY: Your father and I did not fight.

ANGELA: And I suppose when Roberto lived here you didn't fight either?

LUCY: *Mira* what are you trying to do? What do you want from me?

MICHAEL: Look, I hate to break this up, but I'm a little tired.

LUCY: Ah hah, you see, now you've upset your brother. I hope you're happy.

MICHAEL: I'm not upset, Ma, it just was a long trip. I'm gonna go lie down for a while.

ANGELA: Go ahead, even if you're spoiling the party.

MICHAEL: You know something, you haven't changed a bit. You've still got the biggest mouth in the Bronx.

ANGELA: I have so changed. Didn't you notice? I've gotten more fabulous with each day.

MICHAEL: You know, creep, there's a vacant room in the hospital now. I'd be more than happy to give you a recommendation.

ANGELA: Thanks, but no thanks. I'm not ready to chase butterflies yet.

LUCY: Angela . . .

MICHAEL: She's only joking, Ma. Don't be so sensitive. I'm not . . . I'll see you all in a while.

ANGELA: Wait till you see the new curtains *mami* put in your room. (MICHAEL *exits into his room.*)

LUCY: *Malvada. (She follows* MICHAEL *into his room.*) Michael?

MICHAEL: Yeah, Ma?

LUCY: I know before you left something happened between us. I don't know what, but I know that something happened. We stopped talking to each other. We became like strangers. I don't want that to happen again. I love you too much.

MICHAEL: I know, Ma.

LUCY: And Michael, about that hospital . . . please don't hate me for not going to visit you there.

MICHAEL: What are you talking about? How could I hate you? (*He hugs her.*) Hey, you're getting fat in your old age . . .

LUCY: Oh, get out of here . . .

MICHAEL: You haven't been fooling around, have you? Huh, Mama? (*He tickles her and they laugh.*)

LUCY: Oh, shut up . . . (*After a few moments she starts for the door then turns and looks at him softly.*) Michael, I'm sorry about the cake.

MICHAEL: I'm not. I'm allergic to chocolate, remember? (*She exits.* MICHAEL *looks around the room, then sits looking out the window.*)

ANGELA: You see, Ma? I told you there was nothing to worry about. He's fine.

LUCY: Yeah.

ROSA: Damn he looks great. That fresh air must have really done him good. Maybe I'll take him up on that vacant room. I wonder what it could do for me?

SONIA: Probably turn you into a nun.

ROSA: *Ay, fo!* Can you imagine me a nun?

ANGELA: Frankly, no.

ROSA: Ahhh, I don't know. I've heard they've got some pretty wild ones too. I've gotten where I don't trust anybody.

LUCY: Don't talk like that. God is going to punish you.

ROSA: Are you kidding? He's been doing that since the day I was born!

LUCY: Ay, I wish I could stop worrying about Michael.

SONIA: He's fine, Lucy.

LUCY: Yeah. Sonia, *hazme el favor* and go and see if he's okay, will you?

SONIA: Sure. (*She starts toward the room.*)

ROSA: Don't worry so much, Lucy.

LUCY: I know, I know.

ACT ONE

SCENE TWO

The lights dim on the living room. MICHAEL is still seated looking out the window. Somewhere during this next scene LUCY whispers something to ROSA and they exit offstage. SONIA knocks on the door and peeks in.

SONIA: Can I come in?

MICHAEL: Sure. My mother send you in here?

SONIA: How'd you guess?

MICHAEL: I wish she'd stop worrying so much.

SONIA: She can't. She loves you.

MICHAEL: I wish she loved me a little less and helped me a little more.

SONIA: You must be glad to be home.

MICHAEL: Let's say I'm glad to be out of the hospital. Jesus, listening to them out there makes me think that maybe they've got the wrong people locked up.

SONIA: You're telling me.

MICHAEL: *(Half laughing.)* Like the curtains?

SONIA: Yeah, they're kind of nice.

MICHAEL: I swear, Sonia, you are such a hick. They're awful.

SONIA: *(After a pause.)* Hey, what are you gonna do tonight?

MICHAEL: Rest, why?

SONIA: I thought maybe you'd wanna go to a movie or something. Or you know, they have dancing at La Campana now.

MICHAEL: You're kidding? How can they? That place is so small.

SONIA: Not any more. They broke down one of the walls in the back. You should see it. It's really kind of nice.

MICHAEL: Sorry. I don't care if I never see that place again. I can't believe I ever worked there.

SONIA: It's not that bad.

MICHAEL: No? And since when did you start going there. You

never used to hang out there.

SONIA: I've gone with my mother a few times. Besides, there's not too many places to go around here.

MICHAEL: You could always get on a subway.

SONIA: I don't know. I feel kind of funny about going out alone.

MICHAEL: Yeah, I know what you mean. (*Indicates suitcase.*) I better start putting this stuff away.

SONIA: I'll help you.

MICHAEL: (*Starts unpacking.*) So, tell me about this guy Tony. How long's that been going on?

SONIA: I met him pretty soon after you left.

MICHAEL: You mentioned him a few times, but it sounds like it's gotten serious.

SONIA: It has. God, sometimes I don't believe it. I think I really love him.

MICHAEL: Think?

SONIA: Well, I've never really been in love before, so how can I tell?

MICHAEL: If I remember correctly, when you were in junior high school you were in love every two weeks.

SONIA: (*Laughing.*) Please, don't remind me. Remember? Except that I found out most of them were more interested in my mother. Ah, the hell with it, who cares, anyway. That's over with. And this guy Tony is so different. He's not from around here, for one thing. And I don't know . . . he just makes me feel kind of special. Like I'm a lady or something. Like I'm important. You're the only other person who's ever made me feel that way.

MICHAEL: You are important. . . . So, when do I get to meet him?

SONIA: Soon I hope. He's away at school right now. Do you believe, he's going to college in Idaho of all places.

MICHAEL: Idaho?

SONIA: Yeah. He's studying agriculture or something. But he should be getting a break soon. You'll meet him then. He wasn't gonna take any classes in the summer, but we figured he'd graduate faster if he did.

MICHAEL: (*After a pause.*) God, it feels so strange being in this house again. Everything seems so different and yet it seems like nothing's changed. You know I'd almost forgotten what it looked like. What even the street looked like.

SONIA: I don't think I could ever forget what Simpson Street looked like.

MICHAEL: I never thought I could either, but I did. You know I almost even forgot what the city sounded like. I thought my ears were gonna bust on the subway. It was so loud. In the country the loudest thing you heard were the crickets at night. Damn it, just look out of that window, man. It's a bright sunny day and all you can see is grey. Not even the sun can get through all that garbage. Seeing that everyday makes it too easy to forget that any other kind of life can exist. God, Sonia, I don't want to end up like these people around here who sit around all day drinking, trying to find excuses for being alive.

SONIA: Michael, haven't you ever thought about leaving here?

MICHAEL: Are you kidding? Most of my life.

SONIA: Tony and I have talked about maybe moving away from New York too if we get married.

MICHAEL: Don't tell me you're gonna move to Idaho?

SONIA: No way man, not even for Jesus Christ himself will I move there. But somewhere, away from here.

MICHAEL: Well, there ain't exactly too much agriculture on Simpson Street.

SONIA: You're telling me, unless he wants to open up a ceme-tery . . . How come you look so depressed?

MICHAEL: Who's depressed? I'm home again. I'm happy. Right now what I need most of all is another drink.

SONIA: I'll get them. (ROSA *opens the door and stands in the doorway.*)

ROSA: Hey you two, the party's out there . . . Come on,

Michael, dance with me.

MICHAEL: No.

ROSA: Oh, come on, it'll do you good. Sonia, Lucy wants you to go to the store for her . . . (*As* SONIA *is about to object.*) Right now. (*She gives her* LUCY'*s note and some money.*)

MICHAEL: I'll go.

ROSA: Not on your first day back, you won't. No *señor* . . . (SONIA *exits.* ROSA *continues to stare at* MICHAEL *for a long, uncomfortable pause.*) I really missed you, Michael.

MICHAEL: (*Exiting into the living room.*) I missed you, too. (*He takes off the record.*)

ROSA: Good. Now I don't feel like such a fool.

MICHAEL: Sonia told me she's been going to that club with you.

ROSA: Yeah, she's gone a couple of times. But it's different when you're with your daughter than with your friends. Roberto was asking about you. He was real happy you were coming home. He might have a job for you again. He said to drop around.

MICHAEL: I meant it before when I said things had changed for me. I don't want that kind of life anymore.

ROSA: Sure, of course, who does, really? All I meant is you're gonna need a job and money's money.

MICHAEL: Anyway, Rosa, I may have a job. They set up an interview from the hospital. It's to work with kids in a P.A.L. around here.

ROSA: Terrific. Well, I gave you the message. God, I don't believe you already might have a job. That's perfect for you. Here everybody's trying to help, and you've already done it all yourself. That's one of the things I've always liked about you. You never really seemed to need anybody.

MICHAEL: That's what you think.

ROSA: It's true. Even when you were a kid. You always walked around like you were a fucking prince or something. You didn't take shit from nobody. I used to think if I had grown up like you how differently my life would have been.

MICHAEL: My life ain't exactly been too terrific.

ROSA: Yeah, but people always liked you. They always respected you. You could have any girl around here you want. My own daughter follows you around like a puppy dog.

MICHAEL: We're just good friends.

ROSA: Like us? (*He looks at her a moment then turns away.*) And even when you were working at the bar. You always seemed to be there for your pleasure and not anybody else's. And the way the women would come on to you. Man, you had your choice. I never did. Me, if anybody asked me to go home with them it was because either I was the last one there or he was so drunk it didn't matter to him who I was. Yeah, if I had grown up like you things would have been different.

MICHAEL: If you don't like it Rosa, why do you keep going?

ROSA: It's better than being alone. But you wouldn't know that. You've never had to go around sleeping with people just not to feel alone.

MICHAEL: Rosa, Sonia's a good kid. You shouldn't be taking her to that bar. Don't let her mess herself up.

ROSA: You mean don't let her become like me.

MICHAEL: That's not what I said.

ROSA: It's what you meant. Michael, all I'm doing is trying to teach her the rules of the game.

MICHAEL: Not everybody plays by your rules.

ROSA: Bullshit! The streets may be different, the buildings cleaner, but the people are the same. All bastards out to use anybody who'll let them. Damn, I won't die and I won't let my daughter die like my mother, waiting for her man to come home. Shit, what for? Because she loved him? Man, fuck love. It doesn't exist.

MICHAEL: Sonia thinks she's in love with somebody.

ROSA: That guy Tony? I've seen those letters he's written to her. Filled with the same old promises I've heard a hundred times before. The same old bullshit about what a wonderful life they'll have together. Yeah, till he meets somebody else.

MICHAEL: You ever think that maybe he really does love her?

ROSA: Yeah, sure, the same way my father loved my mother. The same way my husband loved me. Men don't know how to love. And women like my daughter just set themselves up for trouble because they don't believe it. They don't realize these bastards just get married to have somebody to keep them clean for their whores outside.

MICHAEL: Your husband must have really hurt you a lot.

ROSA: No, he made me strong. He made me able to survive.

MICHAEL: Surviving is a lot different than living.

ROSA: Not when you're my age.

LUCY: (*Re-enters.*) You hungry yet? There's plenty of food.

MICHAEL: In a little while, Ma. (*The phone rings and* LUCY *answers it.*)

LUCY: (*Into phone.*) Hello? Oh, hello, Fernando. Yes. One minute. Angela! It's Fernando.

ANGELA: (*Re-entering.*) Ay, coño, tell him I'm not here.

LUCY: I already said you were.

ANELA: I told you I don't wanna talk to him.

LUCY: Michael, tell your sister to talk to Nandy.

MICHAEL: Don't involve me in this, Ma.

LUCY: Angela, please.

ANGELA: Ma, will you mind your own business already?

LUCY: *Mira*, don't talk to me like that. This is still my house.

ANGELA: Okay Ma, whatever you say. Whatever you say. (*Into phone.*) Hello? Yeah. Look Nandy, I thought I made it clear I didn't wanna talk to you. No Nandy, don't come over. There's no point to it, that's why! Look, I don't feel too well. I'm not up to an argument. What do you mean come home? I am home, can't you understand that? I'm home! *Coño*, it's more of a home than I ever had with you. Oh, yeah, Nandy, I remember. I remember when I would have done anything to get away from here. Yes. Even marry you, even marry you. *Ay*, please . . . Listen, Johnny has nothing to do with this. Really? Well tell me, do you really think he's the only one you had to live up to? Well what the hell was I supposed to do? Well then . . . *Mira*, if I'm such a fucking bitch why the hell you gotta keep calling? Can't you understand that I've got nothing to say to you and you've got nothing to say that I wanna hear? (*Slams down the receiver.*) Damn it, you're even boring when you argue! Why can't that man just leave me alone!

LUCY: Angela, you shouldn't talk to him like that. (*Phone rings again.* LUCY *goes to answer.*) Let it ring, Ma.

LUCY: *Pero*, Angela . . .

ANGELA: Let it ring! (*After a few more rings the phone stops.*) Damn him!

LUCY: He is still your husband, Angela.

ANGELA: Not according to me.

LUCY: According to law.

ANGELA: On Simpson Street there are no laws.

MICHAEL: Ma, don't get involved. Let her work things out for herself.

LUCY: Michael, you don't understand. You've been away a long time.

MICHAEL: Not that long, Ma.

LUCY: Other people have problems too you know.

MICHAEL: I know that, Ma, but your interfering isn't helping any.

LUCY: Oh, so I'm the villain again.

MICHAEL: Nobody's saying that, Ma.

LUCY: *Dios mío*, I didn't want any fighting today. I wanted everything to be peaceful, to be nice. *Ay*, Angela I told you I didn't want anything to upset your brother today.

ANGELA: Then why did you start?

LUCY: Me? Because I asked you to talk to your husband?

ANGELA: That's right, Ma. I told you I didn't want to.

LUCY: Angela, he loves you.

ANGELA: I don't care, Ma. I just don't care. He's cold, Ma. Can't you understand that? Damn it, Ma, in the four years we're married I've never even felt like he's made love to me. After all that time a woman wants to feel like she's being taken to bed by a man who cares about her. But no, not Nandy. And then he'd turn around and go right to sleep. The hell with whether or not I was satisfied. That wasn't important. He had done me the honor of marrying me. That should have been satisfaction enough.

LUCY: There's more to marriage than just sex. It's something holy. It's a sacrament. It's sacred. It's not something you throw away when you get tired of it.

ANGELA: Oh yeah, sex is so unimportant that's why you and daddy used to fight about it all the time.

LUCY: That's not true, Angela!

ANGELA: Oh no, no. How thick do you think the walls are in this goddamned apartment?

LUCY: ¡*Que no me hables así*!

MICHAEL: Hey come on, the both of you.

ROSA: Just calm down, everybody.

ANGELA: Shit, first with daddy, then with Roberto, damn I always knew when a riot was gonna start. All I'd have to do is start hearing you begging one of them to go to bed with you!

LUCY: (*Slaps her.*) ¡*Embustera*!

MICHAEL: Enough already! Ma, please . . .

LUCY: Michael, I'm sorry, I'm sorry . . . (SONIA *enters from outside carrying a cake box.*) Sonia, you're back. I almost forgot. Michael, look I ordered you another cake. Sonia just went to pick it up. And this one's not chocolate. Welcome home, Michael. Welcome home. (*Blackout.*)

ACT TWO

SCENE ONE

The setting is the same. It is two months later. LUCY, SONIA *and* ELVA *are there. It is early evening and* LUCY *and* ELVA *are in the kitchen area playing bingo. They both have been drinking.* SONIA *looks on.*

LUCY: (*Calling the numbers.*) B 14 . . . G 51 . . . N 45 . . .

ELVA: Bingo!

LUCY: Lemme see. (*Check her card.*) B 14, I 17, N 41 . . . Wait a minute, I didn't call N 41.

ELVA: Yes, you did.

LUCY: I did not! This is already the third time you've done this Elva. Now stop calling bingo when you don't got it. (*To* SONIA.) *Mira ésta*, Bingo! Bingo! Bingo!

SONIA: Need some help, Elva?

ELVA: (*Roughly.*) No!

SONIA: I just asked.

LUCY: Okay, let's finish the game. (*Calling more numbers.*) O 74 . . . B 1 . . . B 4 and after . . . Bingo!

ELVA: Damn, you always win.

LUCY: Some people are just born lucky I guess.

ELVA: Or else they cheat.

LUCY: You calling me a cheater?

ELVA: No. You just call the numbers too fast.

LUCY: No, I don't. You just move your fingers too slow. Come on, let's play again.

ELVA: No. I'm tired of losing.

LUCY: I love games. What else can we do? Let's play something.

ELVA: No, I don't feel like playing nothing.

LUCY: Come on Sonia, why don't you play?

SONIA: No thank you, Lucy. I'm gonna be leaving soon if Michael doesn't hurry up and get home.

LUCY: I can't imagine what's wrong. He's usually home from work by now. (*She enters* MICHAEL*'s room and looks out of the window.*)

SONIA: Did he have a doctor's appointment today?

LUCY: No, he only goes on Tuesdays.

SONIA: And today that I have to talk to him.

ELVA: *Qué desesperación, nena.*

SONIA: You shut up.

ELVA: What do you have to talk to him about anyway?

SONIA: That's none of your business.

ELVA: *Ay, chuse.*

LUCY: (*Re-entering.*) You want a soda or something?

SONIA: No thanks.

LUCY: Well, you're making me nervous just sitting there.

SONIA: Sorry, I didn't mean to.

LUCY: I wish you'd tell me what's on your mind.

SONIA: Nothing.

LUCY: Nothing, huh? That's why you've been sitting there for a half an hour looking like the cat that ate the canary. *M'ija,* I know you better than that. Come on, you can tell me.

SONIA: I'm not saying nothing till I tell Michael.

LUCY: Does your mother know?

SONIA: No. Not yet. So don't say nothing.

LUCY: How can I say what I don't know?

SONIA: Right.

LUCY: Where is your mother anyway? She was supposed to be here early.

SONIA: I don't know. She's been out all day. I figured she was here.

LUCY: No. Well I saw her for a few minutes this morning, but that was it. She said she had some shopping to do.

ELVA: Knowing her, she's probably with the delivery boy.

SONIA: *Mira Elva,* that's my mother you're talking about.

ELVA: So? It's probably the truth. She'd tell it to you herself.

SONIA: Well, she can say it and I can say it, but you can't.

ELVA: Pardon me.

LUCY: *Sí*, Elva, *no hables tanto.* Forgive her Sonia, she's drunk again.

ELVA: I am not drunk.

LUCY: Okay, forgive her Sonia, she's not drunk. Just stupid.

ELVA: (*Gives her a Bronx cheer.*) *Pa ti.*

LUCY: (*Gives her two Bronx cheers.*) *Pa ti dos veces, cabrona.*

SONIA: Well, I'm gonna go see if she's gotten home. Tell Michael I'll see him later.

LUCY: Okay, *m'ija.* I'll see you later. (*Phone rings.*) *Dios mío*, that's Nandy again.

SONIA: Want me to get it?

LUCY: Nah, I'll do it.

SONIA: Okay. See you.

ELVA: Bye, bye. (SONIA *exits.* LUCY *answers the phone.*)

LUCY: Hello? Yes, Nandy. I told you I'd have her call you when she comes in. *Ay*, Fernando, you're getting to sound like a broken record. She left this morning and I haven't heard from her since. Well, calling her every ten minutes isn't gonna make her get home any faster. No Nandy, I have no idea who that guy at the bar was. I swear. *Ay* Nandy you're drunk. *Mira*, I can't talk now. I have some people here. (*She indicates for* ELVA *to talk.* ELVA *can't be bothered.*)

ELVA: *Ay enganche esa mierda ya!* (LUCY *covers the receiver so Nandy can't hear.*)

LUCY: Yes Nandy, I'll have her call you. I promise. (*Hangs up.*) *Qué hombre. Pero* still I feel sorry for him. That daughter of mine. I wish everybody loved me that much. *Bueno pues*, what can you do. Come on Elva, let's play.

ELVA: Nah, not right now.

LUCY: Damn, nobody ever wants to do anything. I can't believe summer's almost gone and I haven't been to the beach even once. I haven't gone anywhere.

ELVA: You're not the only one. Carlos never wants to go nowhere. I ask him and I ask him . . . Carlos take me to the beach, Carlos, please take me to the movies or something, but no, nothing.

LUCY: He really should take you out. You're turning yellow being in the house all day.

ELVA: You're telling me.

LUCY: Roberto was the same way. Not like my husband. My husband, he liked to have a good time. But Roberto, nobody around here even knew we were together. They never saw us together. And remember how I was before. How I was pretty and I had a good figure. God, how I loved to dance. But Roberto, he hated dancing. He hated everything.

ELVA: Maybe you should find yourself somebody else.

LUCY: Nah, I'm too old already. And with my luck I'd get stuck with another creep who doesn't dance. Who doesn't do anything but sit at a bar and drink. You know, Elva, after a while he used to come home so drunk, I couldn't even get him to sleep with me.

ELVA: I never saw him drink that much.

LUCY: I didn't either. At least until he moved in . . .

ELVA: You know, sometimes when I look back on my life, I wonder if it wouldn't have been better if I had been alone.

LUCY: Maybe. I don't know.

ELVA: *Ay*, I'm getting depressed. Come on, let's play again. Only call the numbers slower this time.

LUCY: Okay. (*There is a rhythmic knock on the door.* LUCY *recognizing it, opens the door and* ROSA *enters elaborately clad with long, gold boots to top off her outfit. She also has quite a few drinks under her belt.*) Hi, Rosa.

ROSA: Hello, hello, hello!

ELVA: (*Rising.*) ¡*Me voy pa'l carajo*!

ROSA: *Ay siéntate care peo*! (ELVA *sits back down.*) Tell me, Lucy, is Michael here?

LUCY: No, he hasn't come home yet.

ROSA: Good. I can relax for a minute.

LUCY: What are you talking about?

ROSA: Well, ever since Saint Michael came home it's not like it was before. I feel like I've got an angel hovering over my shoulder telling me how terrible I am. Telling me to repent.

LUCY: He's not that bad. (*Indicating shoes.*) *Pero*, wait a minute! What have you got on?

ROSA: (*Giggling.*) You like? (*She models.*)

LUCY: Those boots are . . . fabulous.

ROSA: Oh, thank you, lovey. I just got them today. (*To* ELVA.) You like? Aren't they sexy?

LUCY: Don't ask her. She's so drunk she'd find a cucumber sexy.

ELVA: Very funny, Lucy.

ROSA: I'm not too old for them, am I?

LUCY: No. You look like a teenager.

ROSA: Ooooh, you're so sweet. (*Kisses* LUCY *on the cheek.*)

ELVA: Oh, sit down already! (ROSA *gives her a dirty look and sits.*)

LUCY: Maybe I'll get a pair of boots like that.

ELVA: I don't like them. They look like *puta's* shoes.

ROSA: *Wátchalo* . . .

ELVA: They do.

ROSA: *Mira*, ugly, I just got here. Don't start.

LUCY: I think they look good.

ROSA: You really like them? I don't look silly? You should see. They had a pair that went all the way up to here. (*She lifts her dress.*)

LUCY: *Mira*, why not show us your bloomers while you're at it.

ELVA: She probably don't wear any. Too much trouble taking them on and off.

ROSA: (*Lifting her dress all the way up in* ELVA*'s face.*) *Mira fea*, yes I wear them.

ELVA: (*Looking at bloomers.*) *Coño*, I've never seen Friday written so big in my life!

ROSA: And today's Friday, right? I change them everyday.

LUCY: Ay, Rosa.

ROSA: Well what if I had an accident? I don't wanna die in no dirty bloomers.

LUCY: I'm sure Saint Peter wouldn't be interested.

ROSA: You never know. A man is a man.

LUCY: (*Blessing herself.*) Forgive her, God. She knows not what she says.

ROSA: (*Laughing.*) Don't worry. I'm only joking.

LUCY: With you it's hard to tell. Well anyway, where were you all day? I expected you here early.

ROSA: (*Smiling.*) I had things to do.

ELVA: From that smile on your face he must have been good.

ROSA: The best. (*To* LUCY.) Maybe you're not interested in my bloomers but those shoe salesmen sure were.

LUCY: Rosa, you can't go nowhere without there being a story.

ROSA: That bad I'm not. Stop taking everything I say so seriously.

LUCY: I just never know when to believe you.

ROSA: I know what you mean. Sometimes I don't know when to believe myself. . . . Well, isn't anybody gonna offer me a drinkie.

ELVA: Get it yourself.

ROSA: As a matter of fact, I will. I don't need nobody to do nothing for me.

ELVA: Hah!

ROSA: ¿Qué es eso de "hah," huh? You wanna see something funny, go look in the mirror.

ELVA: Don't start with me.

ROSA: (*Disgusted.*) Ahhh, you're too ugly to even look at. (ANGELA *enters from the room.*)

LUCY: Well, it's about time you woke up.

ANGELA: Please. What time is it anyway?

LUCY: After six.

ANGELA: Damn.

ROSA: What time you get in?

ANGELA: Who knows? About seven I think.

LUCY: Eight-thirty to be exact.

ROSA: Must have been some date.

ANGELA: Rosa! Those have to be the tackiest boots I have ever seen.

ROSA: You don't like them?

ANGELA: No, I don't like them.

ROSA: I think they're fun. Except for right this minute. They're killing my feet. (*She takes them off.*)

LUCY: There's coffee from this morning.

ANGELA: Thanks, Ma. (*She begins to heat it.*)

LUCY: Fernando's been calling you all day. He wants you to call him.

ANGELA: Ma, please. I just woke up.

LUCY: That's not my fault.

ANGELA: Do you believe he actually showed up at La Campana last night?

ROSA: I didn't see him. But that doesn't mean anything. After one point I couldn't see nothing.

LUCY: He told me. He asked me if I knew who you were with. He kept me up half the night with his phone calls. I finally told him you were asleep and I wouldn't wake you.

ANGELA: Why didn't you tell him the truth?

LUCY: I don't know the truth.

ANGELA: Oh come on Ma, since you're so interested in my life, since you know everything about me, I'm sure you've figured it out.

LUCY: Look, just give him a call like I said you would, okay? I'm tired of you making me into a liar.

ANGELA: Who's asking you to lie? The only thing I've ever asked you for is to mind your own business.

LUCY: *Mira* enough, Angela! Don't talk to me like I'm some garbage from the street. I'm still your mother.

ANGELA: You're a mother all right.

LUCY: ¡*Que ya te dije que te callaras*!

ANGELA: You don't want me to talk to you like that then just stop getting involved in things that don't concern you.

LUCY: This is still my house and you are still my daughter, and everything you do while you are in my house concerns me. And if you don't like it here, nobody's forcing you to stay.

ANGELA: You want me to tell you what you can do with your house?

ROSA: Hey come on, the two of you, calm down.

LUCY: Rosa . . .

ROSA: Rosa nothing, just calm down.

LUCY: *Dios*, what am I gonna do.

ROSA: You're gonna shut up right now, that's what you're gonna do.

ANGELA: I burned the coffee! *Coño*, why can't that man just leave me alone!

LUCY: He loves you, that's why.

ROSA: Lucy . . .

ELVA: *Déjala*. Let her talk to her daughter.

ROSA: Oh, you shut up, too.

ANGELA: I suppose he was drunk again?

LUCY: What do you think? Angela, he's hurt. I don't like to see what he's doing to himself.

ANGELA: And you think I do? Ma, it kills me inside to see what's happening to him, but I can't help that. I can't go back to him like nothing's happened. I can't go back to being like I was before.

LUCY: He was good to you, Angela. He would have given you anything you wanted.

ANGELA: Except everything I needed.

LUCY: And these creeps you go out with from around here can?

ANGELA: Yes.

LUCY: Then you haven't seen Nandy lately. He's become more and more like them everyday.

ANGELA: Please, Ma.

LUCY: Well, isn't that what you wanted him to be? He's drunk and dirty and he smells of the streets. Or doesn't he remind you yet of that guy Johnny or fulano or whoever it was you were with last night, or any other night since you moved back here?

ANGELA: Let's just forget it, okay?

ELVA: Hey Lucy, come on, let's play bingo or something.

ROSA: Oh, go play with yourself.

ANGELA: I need a drink.

LUCY: Before you eat anything . . .

ANGELA: Yes, before I eat anything! (*Makes one.*) Anybody else?

ELVA: Yeah, me.

ROSA: Don't you ever say no?

ELVA: Mind your own business.

ROSA: Oh, shut up and drink.

LUCY: I suppose you're going out again tonight?

ANGELA: You don't stop, do you? Well, okay, yes, as a matter of fact I am going out again tonight. (*To* ROSA.) And before you ask me, yes, I'm going out with that guy you introduced me to last night.

ROSA: Pablito? He's nice.

ANGELA: He's all right.

ROSA: Well, at least he knows how to spend his money.

LUCY: *Mira*, Rosa, I don't want you introducing no men to my daughter.

ROSA: *Ay, cállate ya.*

ANGELA: Yeah, don't start on her now.

ROSA: *Bueno*, Angela, where's Pablito taking you tonight?

ANGELA: I don't know. I figured we'd go to a movie or something first and then over to Club Broadway.

LUCY: Does he know you're married?

ANGELA: Ma, I think everybody in this world knows I'm married, except me.

ROSA: If you do go to the movies you should go and see that picture *Warrior Lady*.

ANGELA: What the hell is Warrior Lady?

ROSA: It's a good movie. It's one of those martial arts things. It's a love story about a Chinese lady whose husband is killed in this small town on their honeymoon. But what nobody knows is that she's the daughter of the greatest kung fu master back in her home town and to get revenge she wipes them all out with her bare hands.

ANGELA: Rosa, that sounds lousy.

ROSA: No, it's good.

LUCY: Yeah, it's good.

ELVA: When did you see it?

LUCY: Rosa and I went the other day.

ELVA: How come you didn't invite me?

ROSA: Because I wouldn't be seen dead walking down the street with you, that's why.

ELVA: Hey, Rosa . . .

LUCY: Oh, come on, she's only kidding, Elva. Calm down.

ELVA: Well, she better be.

ROSA: What was I saying? Oh yeah, it's a very realistic picture. After seeing it I'm even thinking of studying karate or something.

LUCY: Rosa, I can't believe the amount of bullshit that comes out of your mouth.

ROSA: No, it's true. That way I could protect myself in case anybody would try to mug me or rape me.

ELVA: You know, that's not a bad idea.

ROSA: What? Mugging me or raping me?

ELVA: No, studying something like that. Maybe I should, too.

ROSA: *Oye, car'e culo*, if anybody was gonna start with you they'd take one look at your face and be scared to death.

LUCY: *Mira* you two, I've heard enough fighting for one day. Where the hell is Michael? I'm starting to get worried. He's never this late.

ANGELA: Maybe he stopped off for a drink or something.

LUCY: He would have called.

ANGELA: Maybe he found himself a girlfriend. (LUCY *ignores her and goes again to look out of the window.*)

ROSA: By the way, Angela, did you see the guy I left with last night?

ANGELA: No.

ELVA: That's because she didn't leave with nobody.

ROSA: What are you saying now?

ELVA: That you didn't leave with nobody. I saw you walking home alone.

ROSA: *Oye, culona*, You watch me going to the bathroom, too? I did so leave with somebody.

ELVAL: Like hell you did.

ROSA: I did. His name was Mickey. He works in that gas station over by Hunts Point. We even spent the night together. And he wanted to see me again, but I said no. He was just a kid. But he really liked me. But what am I gonna do with a kid? So I told him I was married and that my husband was coming back today.

ELVA: I still say you're lying.

ROSA: *Coño*, I'm not! (LUCY *re-enters.*) You should have seen him, Lucy. He was really nice. He hadn't planned on staying at the bar too long either until he met me. He was still wearing his coveralls and was afraid of getting grease on me every time we danced, I don't know why, but he just fell for me. He said he could even fall in love with me. That's why I lied to him about my husband. *Dios*, was he fabulous!

ELVA: Then maybe you have a twin, 'cause I saw you walking home alone.

LUCY: *Déjala* Elva.

ROSA: Nah, let her talk. She's just jealous 'cause nobody'll look twice at her.

ELVA: I can get any man I want.

ROSA: Any man who's deaf dumb and blind maybe. The only way you've ever gotten anybody is with *brujería*. With voodoo.

ELVA: Shit, maybe you. (*As* MICHAEL *enters.*)

ROSA: *Ay ya! Ya me tienes con el culo inchao con tu jodienda.*

LUCY: Hello, Michael.

MICHAEL: Damn, it's like walking into World War II every time I come through that door.

LUCY: They're only kidding. Nobody's really fighting.

MICHAEL: Yeah, sure.

LUCY: You're home late.

MICHAEL: Yeah, it was a rough day.

LUCY: You wanna eat? Dinner's ready.

MICHAEL: In a little while. I'm too tired to even think about eating. Work was really a bitch today. Those kids ran my ass off. I must be getting old.

LUCY: If you're old where does that put me.

MICHAEL: I don't remember ever having so much energy.

ANGELA: I'm just glad you're home. Ma was about to send the police out looking for you.

MICHAEL: (*To* ROSA.) Is Sonia home?

ROSA: You would know that better than me. You see more of her than I do.

LUCY: She was here before, but she's coming back. She said she's got something important to tell you.

ROSA: *Bueno*, what were we talking about?

LUCY: Nothing Rosa, just forget it.

ROSA: Oh yeah, Elva was being the same pain in the ass she always is.

MICHAEL: Can't you people even get along for two minutes? Do you gotta fight all the time?

ELVA: Everything was fine. Nobody was fighting till she got here.

ROSA: Oh, shut up.

LUCY: The both of you shut up, or I'm gonna throw both of you out of here. Come on, let's just find something nice to talk about. Let's play bingo or something.

ROSA: *A esta hora* she wants to play bingo. *Coño* Lucy, coming here lately is getting to feel more and more like going to church. You gonna give out communion, too? Or is Father Michael here in charge of that?

MICHAEL: You're drunk, Rosa.

ROSA: And you're not, so what does that prove? That supposed to make you better than me?

MICHAEL: Nobody's saying that.

ROSA: No? Like hell!

LUCY: Rosa, please . . .

MICHAEL: Boy, you've really got it in for me today, don't you?

ROSA: *Coño* since you've been back nobody's supposed to drink, go out, do nothing. What are we supposed to do, Michael? Sit around and talk about how beautiful the world is? Well, I can't. And I'm tired of you putting me down because of it!

MICHAEL: Nobody's putting you down.

ROSA: The hell you're not.

LUCY: Forget it already, Rosa. Enough!

ROSA: *Bueno*, it's the truth.

LUCY: I said enough, *ya* . . .

ROSA: Okay, Lucy, you want me to leave, I'll leave, *pero* I'm tired of this.

LUCY: I'm not asking you to leave Rosa.

ROSA: *Coño*, I'm tired of not being able to open my mouth without being afraid this bastard is gonna jump all over me!

MICHAEL: (*Walking towards room.*) Oh, the hell with you, Rosa.

ROSA: (*Calling after him.*) For somebody who hates fighting so much you sure do a pretty good amount of it yourself.

MICHAEL: Rosa . . .

ROSA: Rosa, nothing. You better grow up kid. You wanna live in a world where people don't fight, then you better either go back in the hospital or move to another planet . . .

LUCY: Rosa, *por favor* . . .

ROSA: 'Cause there's no place in this world where people

don't fight.

LUCY: Enough, the both of you. I don't wanna hear another word.

MICHAEL: Of course not Ma, you don't wanna hear nothing. You never have. (*Crosses to his room.*)

LUCY: Michael . . . *Ay* Rosa, you shouldn't talk to him like that.

ROSA: Stop being so overprotective *ya*. He's a man already. Stop treating him like a baby!

LUCY: That's not what I'm trying to do.

ROSA: Isn't it? *Bueno*, it's about time he started facing the facts of life. It's about time both of you did. *Coño*, Lucy, look at how he's got you. You've been a nervous wreck since the day he came home. You don't even have fun anymore. You'd swear he was the head of the house and *coño* you know he doesn't even give you a penny out of what he makes.

LUCY: That's none of your business, Rosa.

ROSA: It is my business. You're my friend, Lucy. We've been friends a long time. I don't like to see him stepping on you.

LUCY: You don't know what you're talking about.

ROSA: You're more afraid of him than you were of your damned husband. He's your son, man, not your lover.

ANGELA: Damn it, Rosa, can't you just shut up for even a few minutes?

ROSA: Okay, okay, don't everybody jump on me. I'm not looking for an argument. Damn it, Lucy, all I mean is somebody should force him to do something, anything. Since he's been home all he does is go to work and come home and complain about everything. And then he just locks himself up in that room.

ELVA: Why does he bother you so much? Like Lucy said, it's none of your business.

ROSA: *Mira*, it is my business because he's got Sonia doing the same thing. Filling her head with all of his bullshit. I'm sorry, Lucy, Michael is your son, but Sonia's my kid and I don't wanna see her get sick too.

LUCY: Michael is not sick anymore. That was all before. He's better now.

ROSA: I just hope so.

ELVA: And since when all of a sudden do you care so much about Sonia?

ROSA: You just shut up, okay?

ELVA: You've never given a damn about her all her life and you know it.

ROSA: *Coño* shut up, you hear me? Just shut up!

ANGELA: Rosa, calm down. Everybody's just had too much to drink.

ROSA: No. I'm not gonna sit here and listen to some drunken bitch tell me I don't love my daughter.

ELVA: You don't.

ROSA: What would you know about it? You can't even have kids!

ELVA: *¡Maricona!*

ROSA: *¡No, la maricona eres tú!*

ELVA: *Vete pa'l* . . .

ROSA: Why the hell do you think Bosco left? He wanted a kid and you couldn't even give it to him. You're not even a woman, Elva!

ELVA: *¡Hija de la gran puta!*

LUCY: Okay, enough! The both of you!

ELVA: Lucy . . .

LUCY: Lucy nothing! Both of you shut up right now!

ELVA: *Coño*, Lucy, this is the last time I come to this house!

LUCY: Fine. Fine. You don't like my house, then get out! Don't come around! Find some other place to free load. Damn it, I'm tired of you coming here to eat and drink and sleep half the time and not once have you ever thought of me . . . about what I would like. I don't know . . . a bottle . . . six lousy beers. No, all you can do is fight!

ELVA: Yes, Lucy, that's all I do. I was always here when you needed me. Whenever you'd tell me Elva do this for me, Elva do that for me. Who even brought Michael to the hospital when he took those pills? Her? No, it was me. You couldn't do it. I even put up with this pig insulting me all the time because I thought you were my friend, *pero* you've been nobody's friend since the day you met her. *Bueno,* you stay with her and your bottle and your six lousy beers because I've had it with you!

LUCY: Elva, sit down. I didn't mean it. I just don't want people around me fighting all the time. If you want to come here and have a good time, fine, wonderful, but if you've gotta fight, I don't need it and I don't want it.

ELVA: Fine, Lucy, and thank you. Thank you very much. (*As she exits.*) Bunch of drunks, *coño!*

LUCY: *¡Ay Díos, qué más!*

ANGELA: You okay, Ma?

ROSA: Don't worry, Lucy. She'll be back tomorrow, like always.

LUCY: You know something, Rosa. I don't care anymore. I just don't care. (*After a moment* ANGELA *goes to* MICHAEL's *room.*)

ACT TWO

SCENE TWO

Angela knocks on the door of MICHAEL's *room.*

MICHAEL: Yeah?

ANGELA: (*Enters.*) You okay?

MICHAEL: I'm fine.

ANGELA: Hey you know, Michael, you shouldn't let them get to you like that.

MICHAEL: What do you care? You probably agree with Rosa.

You're becoming more and more like her every day.

ANGELA: Thank you, Michael. Thanks a lot.

MICHAEL: Angela, you're a young woman, but with what you're doing to yourself you might just as well be Ma or Rosa or Elva or any one of these ladies around here. You don't even think for yourself anymore. All you do is mouth the same excuses they've told you for years.

ANGELA: What the hell are you talking about?

MICHAEL: Listen to yourself sometime . . . (*Mimicking her.*) "Life is bad. I haven't got a chance."

ANGELA: Well, it's the truth.

MICHAEL: It's bullshit is what it is.

ANGELA: Look, I didn't come in here to argue with you. I just . . .

MICHAEL: I'm not arguing with you. I just can't stand to see what's happening to you.

ANGELA: Nothing is happening to me! I'm just not gonna be hurt anymore.

MICHAEL: And so you'll end up just like them out there. You'll end up just like Ma, needing the Rosas of this world because she hasn't got anything else.

ANGELA: I've got something else. I've got my freedom.

MICHAEL: That's why you've become a slave to the bars.

ANGELA: Michael, look at me. What else is there for me? This is my life man, good, bad, or indifferent, it's my life! I like it when guys tell me I'm pretty. I like it when they tell me they love me. For that minute I can believe that somebody cares for me. Even if it's a lie. Even if it's just for a night. But at least I don't feel so alone.

MICHAEL: Those guys don't care about you and you know it. They're just using you.

ANGELA: No more than I'm using them. You should see them at the bar when I go in. How they look at me. How they buy me drinks.

MICHAEL: Drinks, huh? Well, you've paid a pretty expensive

price for your drinks. You've given up your dignity. Your self respect. Your life, man!

ANGELA: Where the hell were you this past year? A hospital or a monastery, huh? Or did you find some secret passageway to heaven? Where have you been that the world hasn't touched you? Or is your head just so fucked up that you've become oblivious to its effects?

MICHAEL: The world has touched me all right. That's why I went into that hospital in the first place.

ANGELA: Well, I don't feel like locking myself up somewhere. I'm in enough of a prison right where I am. At least out there on the streets, in the bars, I can feel alive.

MICHAEL: You're just fooling yourself. That's not living. That's wasting time! You used to want things, Angela. Remember when we were kids . . . how we'd sit on the fire escape and look down and dream about getting away from here . . . Dream about being somebody important?

ANGELA: And that's all they were, man, dreams. Michael, for the first time in my life I am finally seeing things as they really are.

MICHAEL: No, you're not. All you're seeing is what they want you to see. (*Indicates window.*) Simpson Street is not the whole of reality.

ANGELA: If you're born here, it sure is.

MICHAEL: Bullshit.

ANGELA: Keep thinking it as you go and see your psychiatrist every week for the rest of your life.

MICHAEL: Maybe you should try it.

ANGELA: No, thanks. What's he gonna do for me? Shove a lot of pills down my throat? Institutionalize me till I can learn to cope with the world? I am coping with the world. Just look out there, Michael. All of that garbage is real. All of that shit is real. You can't deny it, and if a doctor tells you it's not, he's lying to you, and you're a fool for believing him. (*After a long silence between them* ANGELA *almost laughs.*) Just look at us. We can't even talk to each other anymore without it becoming a fight. I guess Rosa's right about that, too.

MICHAEL: No, man, Rosa's not right about anything. We weren't all born to die here, never having lived. Angela, just think about what you're doing. Believe me, things can change for you.

ANGELA: It's too late, Michael. It's too late for anything.

MICHAEL: Well, I hope not for me. (*Pause.*) Angela, I'm gonna be leaving here . . . (*He takes, out his suitcase and begins packing.*)

ANGELA: Yeah sure, we all say that.

MICHAEL: I mean it. I've been saving up the money I've made to be able to get away from here. I'm going to California.

ANGELA: California?

MICHAEL: Yeah. One of the guys at the hospital was from there and we would talk sometimes. I got a letter from him the other day and he said he was able to set up a couple of job interviews for me out there.

ANGELA: Why didn't you mention any of this before?

MICHAEL: Because I wasn't sure I could go through with it. Even when I picked up my plane ticket I wasn't sure. But walking in through that door today . . .

ANGELA: When are you thinking of leaving?

MICHAEL: Tonight.

ANGELA: What? What did Ma say?

MICHAEL: I haven't told her yet.

ANGELA: What are you waiting for?

MICHAEL: I just didn't know what to say. Why don't you think about coming with me?

ANGELA: Oh, yeah, sure. What the hell would I do in California? And anyway, it'll probably be the same there as it is here.

MICHAEL: No, Angela, it won't be, at least for me. At least I won't feel like I'm trapped in a dirty sewer like I do here.

At least I'll know I tried.

ANGELA: Just don't get your hopes up.

MICHAEL: Why not? I'm tired of not hoping. And even if things don't work out I'll at least have the satisfaction of knowing I didn't die on Simpson Street. (*There is a knock on the front door.* LUCY *opens it.* SONIA *enters.*)

LUCY: Oh, hello, Sonia.

SONIA: Hi. Hi Ma. I'm glad you're here. I've got something important to tell you.

ROSA: Well, I'm waiting.

SONIA: One minute. Lucy, is Michael home yet?

LUCY: Yeah, he's in his room.

ROSA: Where else?

SONIA: (*Calling.*) Michael! Michael!

MICHAEL: In here.

SONIA: Well, get out here. I wanna tell you something.

ROSA: Will you hurry up!

SONIA: Just hold your horses. (*As* MICHAEL *enters followed by* ANGELA.) Damn, I thought you'd never get home from work.

MICHAEL: I had to work overtime. Well, what is it? What's so important?

SONIA: (*Showing a ring on her finger.*) Look!

MICHAEL: Oh, wow, Sonia, that's wonderful! (*He hugs her.*)

LUCY: I knew it. I knew it. Congratulations, *m'ija.*

ANGELA: That's terrific, Sonia. Congratulations.

LUCY: Well, Rosa, aren't you gonna say anything to your daughter?

ROSA: What can I say?

SONIA: Thanks a lot, Ma.

MICHAEL: When did all this happen?

SONIA: Today. I was just sitting home watching television when the phone rang. It was Tony. He had taken his last final and was here at his mother's house. I went over there and he surprised me with this. Isn't it beautiful?

MICHAEL: Yeah!

SONIA: I'm just so happy!

LUCY: You should be. That's wonderful. And you're gonna look so pretty in my wedding dress.

SONIA: I'm sorry, Lucy, but I don't think I'll be using it. We're getting married in City Hall.

LUCY: Another one.

MICHAEL: So when's the big day?

ROSA: Yeah, when do I get rid of you?

SONIA: Well, he's only got a couple of weeks before school starts again, so right away.

ANGELA: How come so fast?

SONIA: He says he can't wait. He thinks I'm gonna find somebody else while he's away so he wants to make sure I don't. Can you imagine me a married lady?

LUCY: Mira, I have an idea. Why don't you call him up and ask him to come over for dinner? That way we can all meet him. (SONIA *hesitating, looks at* MICHAEL; *then at* ROSA *and then back to* MICHAEL.)

SONIA: Well, ah . . . well, we kind of had other plans.

MICHAEL: Yeah, Ma, I'm sure they want to go out and celebrate.

LUCY: I guess I understand, but I'd better meet him before the wedding.

SONIA: You will, Lucy. You will.

ROSA: Don't hold your breath. I haven't met the white knight either.

SONIA: And you might never.

ROSA: You've met one man, you've met them all. (MICHAEL *disgusted, goes into his room.* SONIA *follows him.*)

LUCY: Rosa, you'll never change.

SONIA: (*To* MICHAEL.) Tony figured I could move to Idaho with him till he finishes school.

LUCY: (*To* ANGELA.) You hungry?

ANGELA: No, thanks. (LUCY *begins to serve* ROSA. *She also prepares plates for* MICHAEL *and* SONIA.)

SONIA: He's got an apartment there and everything. It'll be rough at first. He's only got a part-time job, so I'll have to get one, too.

MICHAEL: I thought not even for Jesus Christ would you move to Idaho.

SONIA: Jesus Christ didn't ask me to marry him . . . Can you imagine me a farmer's wife?

MICHAEL: I think it's great!

SONIA: Are you sure? I'm a little scared with everything happening so fast and all.

MICHAEL: You love him, don't you? That's all that's important.

SONIA: But what if he really doesn't love me? What if he's been lying to me? What if it doesn't work?

MICHAEL: But what if it does? You'll never know until you try.

SONIA: Well, I better get ready for tonight. You know, Michael, I was hoping you would come with me.

MICHAEL: No, I don't think so.

SONIA: I think Tony's a little jealous of you. I've talked about you so much.

MICHAEL: Some other time.

LUCY: (*Knocks on the door.*) Hey, come on you two . . .

MICHAEL: Look, I can't really talk right now, but something's come up for me too. I'll tell you about it later. Don't go out till I get there.

SONIA: Okay. (*They exit into the other room.* SONIA *stares at her mother a moment.*) Mommy, haven't you got anything to say to me?

ROSA: (*After a pause.*) I think you're a fool.

SONIA: You know Ma, my whole life you've tried to ruin every thing good for me. Everything good in me. But not this time. This time I won't let you.

ROSA: I won't have to ruin it. He will.

SONIA: Thanks, Ma. Thank you very much. (*She starts to exit, trying to hold back her tears.*)

LUCY: Wait Sonia, she didn't mean that . . . (*But* SONIA *is gone.*) Rosa, how could you say that to her?

ROSA: It's the truth, Lucy. I'm supposed to be happy that she's getting married? Why? So some guy can come and screw up her life even more?

MICHAEL: You really can't believe in love, can you?

ROSA: Not from a man.

MICHAEL: You just can't stand to see anybody who's not like you. It kills you to think that maybe somebody could be happy.

ROSA: I've survived a hell of a lot longer and a hell of a lot better than you, so don't you tell me about my problems.

MICHAEL: Yeah, you've survived, by destroying everybody that comes near you.

ROSA: Drop dead.

MICHAEL: What is it you want Sonia to do? Sit home and become like you?

ROSA: She could do worse.

LUCY: Please. The both of you . . .

MICHAEL: How, Rosa? What's worse than having no life? Than having to invent people who love you? Than having nobody who gives a damn about you, including yourself?

ROSA: There are plenty of people who love me.

LUCY: Stop it! Come on.

MICHAEL: You're so bitter Rosa, you've forgotten what it is to love. (*Starts for his room.*)

ROSA: You think you know so much and you don't know nothing. That's right baby, go lock yourself up in your room again. You know, I think somebody forgot to tell you you came out of the hospital. I think you think you're still there.

MICHAEL: Sometimes I wish I was.

ROSA: You're not the only one.

LUCY: Rosa, *¡déjalo!*

MICHAEL: Go to hell, lady, just go to hell. (*He goes into*

his room.)

LUCY: *Coño*, Rosa, how can you talk to him like that?

ROSA: Everything I said was the truth. And just be careful that he doesn't end up back in the hospital again.

LUCY: Don't say that! He is not sick anymore. And I never want to hear you say that again. Do you understand?

ROSA: *Mira,* Lucy . . .

LUCY: Lucy, nothing! *Oyeme,* Rosa, you may be my friend, but Michael is my son, and he comes first.

ROSA: Well, maybe it's about time he didn't.

LUCY: *Carajo* Rosa, I don't want to hear another word!

ROSA: Wonderful Lucy, terrific. Have it your way. (*Starts to exit.*)

LUCY: Rosa, where are you going now?

ROSA: *Pa'l carajo,* Lucy! *Pa'l carajo!*(*Exits.*)

LUCY: *Dios mío, qué vida . . . qué vida.*

ANGELA: (*After a long pause.*) I'd better get dressed. (*She exits. LUCY sits there not knowing what to do, then looks towards MICHAEL's room, a worried look crossing her face as if she senses something. After a long moment she rises and goes towards MICHAEL's room and begins knocking on the door.*)

LUCY: Michael? Michael? (*He quickly closes the suitcase and takes it off the bed.*)

MICHAEL: One minute. (*He opens the door and LUCY enters.*)

LUCY: Everything okay in here?

MICHAEL: Yeah Ma, everything's fine.

LUCY: Good. (*Starts to leave.*)

MICHAEL: Ma, don't go yet. I'd like to talk to you a minute.

LUCY: Look Michael, I know what you're gonna say and I'm really sorry about what happened inside just now. You shouldn't let Rosa bother you like that.

MICHAEL: It's not about that, Ma.

LUCY: It really hurts me to see you like this.

MICHAEL: To see me like what?

LUCY: So upset and everything.

MICHAEL: Forget about it, Ma.

LUCY: I can't forget it. I'm trying to do what's right for you. I'm trying to understand you. I really am.

MICHAEL: I know, Ma.

LUCY: Why don't you have your dinner? Nobody'll bother you, Michael. Rosa's not even here anymore. She left. She went home.

MICHAEL: Till tomorrow.

LUCY: Don't mind her so much, Michael. She's not really bad. She talks stupid and crazy sometimes, but she doesn't mean to hurt anybody.

MICHAEL: It's not important now.

LUCY: Michael! I just get so afraid. You've changed so much. Sometimes I feel you don't even love me anymore.

MICHAEL: You know I do, Ma.

LUCY: No, I don't. We don't share anything anymore. We don't even talk to each other anymore. Remember when you were a little boy? There was nothing we couldn't say to each other. Now most of the time you don't even wanna try. I've lost you. (MICHAEL *looks at her a moment, not being able to answer.*)

MICHAEL: Ma, there's something I have to tell you. I've been putting it off for a long time, but I can't anymore.

LUCY: Michael, what is it? (MICHAEL *takes a plane ticket from the dresser drawer.*)

MICHAEL: This is why I was late today, Ma. I went to pick this up.

LUCY: A plane ticket. Michael, what is this? Are you going some place?

MICHAEL: I'm moving out, Ma.

LUCY: What?

MICHAEL: I'm leaving. I'm going to California.

LUCY: California?

MICHAEL: Yeah.

LUCY: (*Staring at the ticket.*) Michael, there's got to be a mistake. This ticket says for tonight.

MICHAEL: I know, Ma. I'm sorry to tell you this way, but I couldn't think of how else to do it.

LUCY: Michael, I don't believe this. Just like that you're going to California? You couldn't even discuss it with me?

MICHAEL: There's nothing to discuss, Ma.

LUCY: Oh, no, of course not. Why tell me anything? I'm nobody to you. Just your lousy son of a bitch of a mother, right?

MICHAEL: Ma . . . (*Pulling suitcase out and placing it on the bed.*) I'd better finish packing.

LUCY: How long have you been planning this? I can't believe this. You're not doing this to me, Michael. You can't hate me that much.

MICHAEL: I don't hate you, Ma.

LUCY: Then why are you trying to hurt me like this? Michael, what are you gonna do in California? You don't belong there. Who do you even know there?

MICHAEL: Ma, you've always tried to understand me, so please, try to listen to me now . . .

LUCY: No, that's not you talking. It's those damned doctors of yours. That damn psychiatrist you see. Did he tell you to leave? Did you tell him what a miserable mother I was? Did he put you up to this?

MICHAEL: This is my own decision. It's something I've got to do for myself. There's nothing for me here. I just don't belong here anymore.

LUCY: No, of course not. You're too good. But it's fine for me to stay here. All of this garbage is good enough for me! Michael, you're gonna walk out on me just like your father did. You're gonna leave me alone, just like he did. I thought you were different Michael, *pero coño,* you're all the same. You're all heartless. You should all die! (*She exits into the living room. MICHAEL follows her.*)

MICHAEL: Ma . . .

LUCY: Michael, what have I ever done to you to deserve this? Why are you so angry with me?

MICHAEL: I'm not . . .

LUCY: Stop it, Michael! Stop it right now! Is it because I didn't go to the hospital? Because I didn't visit you?

MICHAEL: It's got nothing to do with that.

LUCY: That's it, isn't it? Isn't it, Michael? I apologized. I'm sorry. Try to understand. Don't be mad at me for it. I could not see you there! Sure I could have taken a train or a bus and gotten there, but what would have happened to me once I got inside . . .

MICHAEL: I know how much all of that hurt you, Ma.

LUCY: No, you don't know! You'll never know what it's like for a mother to come home and find her son lying here on the floor half dead! My God, I wanted to die, too. I was scared and I was hurt and I didn't understand. My son, who I loved more than myself, would rather be dead!

MICHAEL: That's ancient history now. That's all over with.

LUCY: No, it's not over. It'll never be over to me, I blamed myself for what happened, Michael, I still blame myself for it, but I don't know for what. I still have nightmares about it! I loved you and I always tried to do what was right for you and I failed. I made mistakes, but Michael, I didn't do it on purpose. Why do you keep punishing me?

MICHAEL: I'm not trying to.

LUCY: I didn't set out to hurt my kids. I didn't do it on purpose.

MICHAEL: I'm not blaming you. I'm not accusing you. What's past is past, I've got to deal with the present now.

LUCY: What present? You have a home here and a family and a mother that loves you. That's the present. Michael, I don't even ask you for anything.

MICHAEL: Only that I stay here.

LUCY: Not forever. I just want you to think about it.

MICHAEL: I have thought about it. If I don't do it now, I'm afraid I'll never do it.

LUCY: Think a little about me! Don't be so selfish! I gave up everything for you kids! It was hard trying to be both a mother and father to you after your father left! But I always did what I thought was best. I could have been like one of these women around here and put you in a home and forgotten all about you, but no, I couldn't! *¡La gran pendeja no pude!* I should have goddamned it! This wouldn't be happening to me now if I did!

MICHAEL: Ma, can't you understand that I have my own life to live?

LUCY: Then live it! Because I could never live mine! Even with Roberto. You didn't like him and so I got rid of him. I did it to please you, but you don't understand that, do you?

MICHAEL: I do and I'm sorry.

LUCY: The hell you're sorry!

MICHAEL: Ma, I can't decide your life for you the same way you can't decide my life for me.

LUCY: (*Hitting him with all her fury.*) You decided my life years ago, you bastard! I sacrificed every chance I had in life because of you!

MICHAEL: Yeah, Ma, but that doesn't mean you own me. (*She stares at him a moment, then sits, looking away from him.*) Look Ma, I'll write to you. And if things work out for me maybe you could even come out there and . . .

LUCY: Michael?

MICHAEL: Yeah, Ma . . .

LUCY: Get out. I don't want to see you again. You're not my son.

MICHAEL: Ma . . .

LUCY: Get out. (*He stares at her a moment as she sits looking away from him. He then goes to his room and gets his suitcase. ANGELA has come on, dressed for the evening and stares silently at her mother. MICHAEL re-enters the room.*)

ANGELA: Good luck, Michael.

MICHAEL: Thank you. (*He hugs her.*) See that she's okay.

ANGELA: Yeah, sure . . . (*He starts to exit, but stops and looks at his mother.*)

MICHAEL: *¿Bendición Mamá?* (*She stares away from him, silently. After another moment he exits.*)

ANGELA: Come on, Ma, everything's gonna be okay.

LUCY: (*After a long pause.*) He left. I don't believe it. He left. Just like his father. *Coño,* they're all the same. (*She starts to break; however, the strength of her survival also shows through.*) One day it's gonna be me who leaves here. I swear it! One day you're gonna come to the door and not find me. It's time, *coño,* that I had a life of my own. You're gonna see. One day I'm gonna pack up my bags and disappear. And nobody's ever going to see me again. One day I'm gonna be the one who walks out. I'm gonna be the one who leaves.

Slow blackout

Waltz on a Merry-Go-Round

by

Edward Gallardo

(Incidental Music by Bruce J. Taub)

Dedicated to Silvana Gallardo, Bruce J. Taub,
and Brooke Cadwallader for their belief and support
during the creation of this work.

Characters:

SARA (RIVERA) MONTGOMERY: A strong, handsome
woman in her early thirties, battered by time and an unhappy
marriage. She finds solace in her memories as her present is bleak
and her future tenuous; yet she is not prone to self-pity and
dislikes it in others. She is a survivor of the ultimate kind, hiding
all traces of her vulnerability, even if the result often manifests
itself in anger.

JASON MONTGOMERY: Sara's husband. He is an ex-
tremely good-looking man in his mid-thirties. He has a powerful
body, developed by years of working the fields. He is slow,
deliberate, and calculating and moves with the sensuality of a
panther aware of its strength and beauty. He has been blessed, or
cursed, with the charm of seduction, often casting a hypnotic
effect on others, even in his silences.

ISABELLA: Sara's older sister and her arch rival. She is a
high-strung woman in her mid-thirties who at first sight appears
quite fragile; however, she can be quite resilient. She is nervous,
overwrought, and equally defensive and can turn from a lamb
into a lioness at a moment's notice. She hates the fact that she is
Hispanic, almost as much as she does Sara. She prides herself on
her education and on being "Daddy's favorite."

MIRIAM: Sara's youngest sister. She is a seventeen year-old girl who alternates between fantasy and reality, so can appear quite child-like or womanly, depending on the moment. Her friends are the dolls she plays with. Her favorite is a rag doll named Amanda whom she speaks to constantly.

EVELYN: Sara's twenty-four-year-old sister. She is quite casual about her appearance and personality, so no one would suspect her many complexes or feelings of inadequacy. She is a poet who has to work as a receptionist to support herself. Although she ran away to the city, she loves Sara deeply and feels more like a daughter to her than a sister.

CARMEN: Another sister. She is twenty-eight years old and has been pregnant most of her adult life. She is fun-loving, and sweet, but has the mouth of a truck driver and is very different from the others. She loves her sisters and tries to mediate their quarrels; however, she joins right in when her own temper takes over. She is very much in love with her common-law husband, Luis, and is proud of his accomplishments, no matter how slight they might seem to others.

LUIS MARTINEZ: Carmen's husband. He is a simple man in his early thirties who likes driving and working with his hands. He, too, loves Carmen, although she does have a knack for embarrassing him. He is a good father to her kids and treats them as his own. He can be easily impressed but is not envious of others, as he is satisfied with his life.

JOSEPHINE WILSON: A slovenly woman in her fifties with a person ality as abrasive as her permanent scowl, who resides at the Montgomery Guest House.

HENRY WILSON: Josephine's husband. He is a sweating, fifty-three-year-old, out-of-work redneck, with a soft body and lots of opinions. Although he tries to bluster a lot, he is easily dominated.

MR. LUKAS: An elderly, religious black gentleman, whose memory has faded with his youth. He, too, is a boarder at the Guest House as his wife has left him and his only son lives in New York City.

ACT ONE

SCENE ONE

Before a cyclorama, dark fast-moving rain clouds pass over the Montgomery Guest House; a lonely whitewashed, wooden boarding house located on the outskirts of VanHornesville, a small, forgotten town near Starkville, in upstate New York. Visible are the parlor, front porch and a small parcel of the land leading up to it.

The parlor is cluttered with overstuffed chairs and tables filled with family mementos. A swinging door, USL, leads to the kitchen and on a table nearest to it sit a large coffee urn, cups and saucers, and a plate of homemade biscuits. There are also a bar and a phonograph in the room, next to which stand a small assortment of records. In one corner of the room is a large collection of dolls, the largest being a rag doll named Amanda.

SR, an archway leads to the guest rooms and US, a staircase leading to the rooms occupied by the owners. The porch is bare, except for a swing on which a morning newspaper and a pair of dentures are placed.

In the darkness the sound of thunder is heard, soon joined by the sound of rain. A dark, haunting waltz filters in. The passing rain clouds have done nothing to cool off the hot, humid, early June morning and the air hangs thick and oppressive. The music we hear is coming from the phonograph in the parlor, where at present an assortment of cleaning items, such as furniture polish, rags, a broom and dust pan, etc, are scattered about. A laundry basket filled with soiled clothing is placed off to the side.

SARA is standing on the porch, a distant look on her face as she gazes off into the horizon. An untouched cup of coffee sits on the railing in front of her. She has been working in the house all morning and the sweat on her back can be seen staining through her simple, cotton dress. After a few moments the tele-

phone rings, jolting her back to reality. She takes a sip of her coffee before entering inside to answer it.

SARA: (*Into phone.*) Hello? No, I'm afraid Jason's not ... (*Then as if already knowing the answer.*) Who is this? I thought I told you never to call my home. I don't give a damn what Jason said. Don't do it again! (*She slams the receiver and stands looking down at the phone.* JASON, *her husband since childhood, enters from upstairs dressed only in his pajama bottoms.*)

JASON: Who was that on the phone just now?

SARA: Edna. She said you told her to call.

JASON: Oh hell, I forgot.

SARA: You seem to forget a lot of things! (JASON *gets himself a cup of coffee and sits massaging the awakening muscles in his neck.* SARA *continues with her housekeeping; however, the tension between the two is as thick as the humidity.*)

JASON: (*After a pause.*) Don't you find your choice of music a bit morbid for the morning?

SARA: I wasn't playing it for you.

JASON: I am well aware of that, Sara. Forgive me for interrupting your requiem. (*Another pause.*) Poor Michael, gone but not forgotten. (SARA *takes off the record as if the mere mention of Michael's name from* JASON *is offensive to her. She stands watching* JASON *a moment.*)

SARA: I didn't think you'd be up this early. In fact, from the condition you came home in, I thought you'd sleep all day.

JASON: Good morning to you, too, Sara.

SARA: Put some clothes on. People will be up in a minute.

JASON: Considering the high class clientele that infests this place, I'm sure nobody'd give a damn.

SARA: Well, I do! I don't want you parading around half-naked in front of my sister!

JASON: Can I at least finish my coffee, or is that asking for too much?

SARA: (*Throwing a shirt at him from the laundry basket.*) Put on some damned clothes first!

JASON: Why do I get the feeling this is going to be a wonderful day? (*He puts on the shirt, leaving it unbuttoned.*)

SARA: What did you want to talk to Edna about?

JASON: Nothing much. We've just got a little business deal going.

SARA: Business . . . Is that what you call it? Jason, I thought you were through with all that.

JASON: Apparently not.

SARA: That's you, Jason. Always plotting. Always scheming.

JASON: Jesus, what the hell is it with you this morning?

SARA: Nothing. Absolutely nothing! (*After a slight pause.*) Is that where you were all night? At Edna's?

JASON: You know better than to ask questions you don't want the answers to.

SARA: Jason . . .

JASON: All right! I drove over to Starkville. I met some of my buddies for a drink!

SARA: Who? Henry inside and the rest of the parasites you seem to enjoy supporting?

JASON: It is too damned hot to be listening to your mouth right now! Can we postpone all this till a little later?

SARA: No, Jason, we cannot postpone all this till a little later!

JASON: Well, I don't feel like hearing it right now!

SARA: I don't give a damn what you feel like!

JASON: Quit ordering me around! I am not still that dirty little kid working for your father! (JOSEPHINE *enters from inside.*)

JOSEPHINE: Will you two keep it down in here? Some of us do like to sleep in the morning.

SARA: Move if you don't like it.

JOSEPHINE: Listen you, I pay rent here.

SARA: Good. It's due today. As it has been for the past three weeks.

JOSEPHINE: It's not my fault Henry lost his job at the bank . . . that bastard Jed fired him for no good reason. Besides, Jason said it was all right for us to stay until Henry found another one.

SARA: Oh, did he now?

JASON: Is Henry up yet?

JOSEPHINE: Who knows? He didn't come home last night. I was just about to ask if you knew where he was.

JASON: Sorry, Josephine.

JOSEPHINE: He's the one who's gonna be sorry when he finally shows his face.

SARA: I just hope wherever he is, he's making some money.

JOSEPHINE: Oh, go to hell.

SARA: After you, lady, after you. (JOSEPHINE *exits.*)

JASON: Now is that any way to talk to our guests?

SARA: Who does she think she is talking to me like that? I own this damned place.

JASON: Correction, Sara. I own it. But at the rate you go through boarders, maybe not for too much longer.

SARA: I wish they would move. I wish they'd all move. I wish this whole damned house would burn down again!

JASON: If you'll excuse me . . .

SARA: Where the hell do you think you are going?

JASON: To take a shower. Or do I need your permission for that, too?

SARA: Just make sure you wash off whatever whore you contaminated last night.

JASON: Why? She was so lovely. In fact she looked a little like you. Younger, of course.

SARA: Jason, your little descriptions don't bother me anymore, so don't try. (JASON *starts to exit, but turns back to her.*)

JASON: It's funny, the whole time we were together I kept thinking how much Michael might have enjoyed her, too. (He exits.)

SARA: Bastard. (*She continues working a moment, then realizes the time.*) Miriam? Miriam? Aren't you up yet?

MIRIAM: (*Offstage.*) I'll be right down. (*She enters carrying a blue feather boa. She goes to the dolls and kisses Amanda.*) Good morning, Amanda.

SARA: You talk to her more than you do me.

MIRIAM: (*Putting the boa on the doll.*) Look what I've got for you. Isn't it pretty?

SARA: Where did you find that?

MIRIAM: In the attic . . . You look terrible.

SARA: Thanks.

MIRIAM: I could hear you arguing with Jason. You shouldn't be so hard on him.

SARA: And you should mind your own business. You're starting to sound like Isabella.

MIRIAM: What time did he come home last night?

SARA: I don't know. Somewhere between Claudette Colbert in the Philippines and the Sermonette. Damn, I'm going blind watching so much television. I wish I could sleep.

MIRIAM: I didn't sleep well either. I kept having bad dreams.

SARA: I know. I could hear you. (MIRIAM *takes a sip from a cup of coffee she has poured.*)

MIRIAM: This coffee's rotten.

SARA: Then don't drink it.

MIRIAM: (*As she adds heaping spoonsful of sugar to her cup.*) I kept dreaming they wanted to put me away and that you let them. They put me in a room with all these crazy people . . . It was terrible. Amanda didn't like it either. Would you let them put me away if they tell you to again?

SARA: Stop talking nonsense.

MIRIAM: Are you sure I don't bother you?

SARA: Honey, if that was the case I would have put you away a long time ago. And your sister, Isabella, right behind you.

MIRIAM: You don't like her much, do you?

SARA: What's there to like?

MIRIAM: Do you like any of them better than me? Carmen or

Evelyn, I mean.

SARA: Will you hurry up and get ready for school?

MIRIAM: It's not a school. It's a Wack-O Center. Do I have to go today?

SARA: Don't start this again. There's only a couple of days left before summer vacation.

MIRIAM: All I ever do is sit around watching a bunch of retards acting stupid.

SARA: How many times have I told you not to use that word? They are not retarded. They're emotionally upset.

MIRIAM: I am emotionally upset. They are retarded.

SARA: What's this all about, Miriam?

MIRIAM: Nothing.

SARA: I know you too well, so just get it over with.

MIRIAM: (*After a pause.*) Miss Margolis wants you to come in today.

SARA: Don't tell me you're in trouble again?

MIRIAM: Why do you always think it's for something bad?

SARA: Isn't it?

MIRIAM: Yes, but it didn't have to be. I could have done something good.

SARA: Just tell me what happened?

MIRIAM: Nothing, really.

SARA: Miss Margolis wouldn't want to see me if it was for nothing.

MIRIAM: Well, it really wasn't my fault! I just had a fight, that's all.

SARA: Again? Jesus Christ, when are you going to learn? I haven't got time to be going to school for you everyday.

MIRIAM: You don't have to go everyday.

SARA: No? Between all your fighting and playing hookey, I'm in school more for you now than I was for myself.

MIRIAM: Then don't go. I'll tell her you're too busy.

SARA: What was the fight about? Miriam, I asked you what the fight was about?

MIRIAM: This balloon head in my class started making fun of me because I'm older than the rest. She started laughing at me and telling everybody that I was crazy.

SARA: And . . .

MIRIAM: And so I pushed her down the stairs.

SARA: My God, Miriam, what is wrong with you? Is she all right?

MIRIAM: She's fine . . . Except I think she broke her arm.

SARA: Oh, that's just wonderful. Damn it, you know what they told me the last time.

MIRIAM: She shouldn't have said I was crazy.

SARA: I don't know if I blame her, the way you act sometimes. Fighting and all your damned dolls . . . (*She goes to take Amanda from her, but* MIRIAM *screams.*)

MIRIAM: No! (*She holds the doll close.*)

SARA: (*After a slight pause.*) I'm sorry, Miriam. I didn't mean that.

MIRIAM: They're my friends.

SARA: You should be out trying to make real friends. (MR. LUKAS, *enters from his room.*)

LUKAS: Good morning, ladies.

SARA: Good morning, Mr. Lukas.

MIRIAM: You left your teeth on the porch again last night. (SARA *shoots her a look.*)

LUKAS: Did you happen to see my Bible, Miss Sara? I couldn't say my morning prayers today.

SARA: (*As she gives him a cup of coffee and a biscuit.*) I'm sure God will forgive you this one time, Mr. Lukas. I left the morning paper outside for you. I know how much you like to sit out there.

LUKAS: Biscuits look good. I think I'll have it outside on the porch today for a change. Have you seen the newspaper, Miss Sara? Well, never mind. These old eyes can hardly see anyway. It sure looks like it's gonna be a nice day after all that rain we had yesterday.

MIRIAM: It didn't rain yesterday. It rained this morning.

SARA: Shhhh . . .

LUKAS: It sure looks like it's gonna be a nice day indeed. A little too hot maybe. (*He exits out onto the porch, surprised to find his teeth there, which he places in his mouth.*)

MIRIAM: And people say I'm crazy.

SARA: He's old. He just doesn't remember too good.

MIRIAM: At least he remembered to zipper his fly. Amanda saw his skinny old thing sticking out the other day. She almost fainted.

SARA: Go inside and have some breakfast. I left the Corn Flakes on the table.

MIRIAM: I don't like Corn Flakes.

SARA: Eat them anyway. (*She exits onto the porch. MIRIAM enters the kitchen.*) Did you sleep well, Mr. Lukas?

LUKAS: At my age that's about all you can do well . . . Sleep . . . These biscuits, did you bake them yourself?

SARA: The same as I do every morning.

LUKAS: There's nothing like fresh baked biscuits to start the day.

SARA: (*After a pause.*) I hate to bring this up so early, Mr. Lukas, however, did you find your check?

LUKAS: Check?

SARA: Yes. The one from your son. I usually cash it for you, remember? The rent, it's due today.

LUKAS: Oh, yes. Well, I know I put it somewhere. I just can't remember where that is. Maybe I left it with my Bible. I'm sorry, Miss Sara . . .

SARA: Don't worry, Mr. Lukas. It's happened before. I'm sure it will turn up later on.

LUKAS: Thank you, Miss Sara. You're a fine lady. Your daddy would have been proud of you. (MIRIAM *reenters the parlor and sits eating her cereal with Amanda, opening a small music box on the table next to her. The music it plays is the same as we heard on the record. SARA enters the house and closes the box.*)

SARA: What have I told you about eating in here?

MIRIAM: Nobody can see me. Besides, Amanda doesn't like to eat in the kitchen.

SARA: The hell with what Amanda likes and doesn't like.

MIRIAM: You're just in a bad mood because Jason came home drunk.

SARA: And you're gonna be in a worse mood if you don't hurry up and do what I say! (MIRIAM *starts to obey.*)

MIRIAM: Oh, could you pick some flowers today from the garden? It's Amanda's birthday today.

SARA: Dolls don't have birthdays.

MIRIAM: She likes the roses.

SARA: Well you tell her, the day she starts paying rent here, she can have all the roses she wants. (*Picking up the laundry basket.*) I'll be out back doing the laundry you promised to do yesterday. If I don't see you before you leave, tell Miss Margolis to expect me about twelve-thirty.

MIRIAM: Please, Sara? Please pick the flowers?

SARA: All right, all right! I'll pick her a bunch of damned roses! You're not going to shut up about it till I do. (*She exits inside.*)

MIRIAM: Did you hear that, Amanda? She's going to pick some roses for you. And she's not going to let them put us away. Aren't you happy? Isn't that a nice birthday present? I've got you another present too, Amanda. But you have to turn around and not peek. (*She sets Amanda down and takes a male doll from the group and brings it back to her.*) Okay, you can look now. (*She holds the dolls face to face.*) I got you a boyfriend, Amanda. His name is Johnny. Isn't he handsome? Oh, come on, Amanda, stop being silly. You see, Johnny, she's never been with a man like I have. I like it. Sometimes I let all the boys in school . . . Well, not the fat ones. We sneak down into the basement when nobody's looking. You should try it, Amanda. You should let

Johnny . . . Oh, don't be such a baby. It won't hurt . . . At least when you get used to it. Be gentle, Johnny, remember it's her first time. (*She places Johnny on top of Amanda and moves them in a sexual manner.*) There, what did I tell you? Doesn't it feel good? I told you there was nothing to be afraid of . . . No, Johnny . . . Not yet. A woman takes longer than a man. (JASON *has entered unnoticed by her.*)

JASON: (*After a pause.*) What are you doing?

MIRIAM: (*Quickly separating the dolls.*) Nothing.

JASON: Where's your sister?

MIRIAM: Out back. Jason, do you really mean all those things you tell me?

JASON: What things?

MIRIAM: Like when you tell me I'm pretty and everything?

JASON: Of course I mean them.

MIRIAM: I wish I didn't have to go to school today. I wish you and I could do something together . . . Do whatever you want?

JASON: I'd like that, honey, but I couldn't today either. There's some important business I've got to take care of.

MIRIAM: I had another fight in school, Jason. Miss Margolis wants to see Sara again.

JASON: Why's a pretty girl like you fighting all the time?

MIRIAM: I can't help it. Sometimes those morons get me so mad I could die.

JASON: I know what you mean. Kids can be the cruelest of animals.

MIRIAM: You understand me so well, Jason. At times I think you're the only one who does. Maybe 'cause you used to get into a lot of fights yourself. Though I don't know how anybody could make fun of you.

JASON: You'd be surprised how funny poverty can be to some people. Sometimes I'd hide out in the barn or the apple orchard all day just not to hear their voices. Not hearing anything but the voice inside my head telling me to be strong . . . Not to pay attention to those fools.

MIRIAM: There's no place for me to hide now. Except maybe up in the attic . . . But by now everybody knows where to look.

JASON: You should have seen this place before they built the highway through to Starksville. Before your father sold off everything but this house. My folks and I worked our backs off year round to keep it going. To keep your father the big man he loved pretending to be.

MIRIAM: I'm sorry, Jason. I'm sorry if my father was cruel to you.

JASON: I'm not, because his old bones must be turning in their grave . . . whatever soul he had, at war with his God, for allowing me to right his wrong . . . I remember thinking some days the dirt on our skin would never wash clean . . . That it had dug its way so deep inside it had become part of our blood. Blood your father felt free to spill in his alcoholic binges . . . And always making sure it was in the company of others so that our humiliation was public, unquestionable, and totally complete. That's why I took my mother away from here soon after my father died. And it's also why I came back after yours did.

MIRIAM: Is that when you met up with Edna? When you left here?

JASON: What do you know about Edna?

MIRIAM: I've heard Sara talk. And I've heard others talking about her, too.

JASON: That's because the fine people of this town have nothing better to do than gossip. Edna's a good woman. Took good care of my mother and anyone else who needed. She treated her with respect, even though she worked cleaning up after her girls for her. And God help anyone else who didn't. Without Edna I'd be like everyone else in this town . . . out of work . . . out of hope . . . and filled with envy over people like me and her now.

MIRIAM: If she's so good, Jason, why does she run that kind of house? Why'd Lukas try to have her run out of town like I heard?

JASON: Because Lukas's wife preferred the sanctity of Edna's to the rambling hypocrisy of a pious old fool, that's why. (SARA *enters.*)

SARA: You still haven't left yet?

MIRIAM: I'll be ready in a minute.

SARA: Make it thirty seconds. The school bus has probably come and gone by now.

MIRIAM: Jason will drive me, won't you Jason?

JASON: Sure, honey, whatever you want. (MIRIAM *exits.*) I can't seem to find my blue shirt, Sara. Did you happen to see it anywhere?

SARA: As a matter of fact, I did. I cut it up for rags yesterday. Now, is there anything else?

JASON: No, Sara, at least for now. (*He exits.* SARA *takes the broom and dustpan from the corner and exits into the kitchen as* EVELYN, SARA's *twenty-four-year-old sister enters onto the porch carrying a small suitcase.*

EVELYN: Hello, Mr. Lukas, remember me?

LUKAS: (*Looks up startled from his paper.*) Can't say that I do.

EVELYN: I'm Evelyn, Sara's sister.

LUKAS: Who?

EVELYN: Never mind. It's not important. (*She enters the house and* LUKAS *returns to his newspaper; however, he shortly falls off to sleep.*) Sara? Sara?

SARA: (*Offstage.*) Evelyn? (*She enters, having been in the middle of cooking.*) Evelyn! What in the world are you doing here! (*They embrace.*)

EVELYN: You mean you didn't know? I thought Jason was kidding when he said he wanted to surprise you.

SARA: Jason? What does Jason have to do with anything?

EVELYN: He called and asked me to come up. As far as I know we're all gonna be here. Me, Carmen, Isabella.

SARA: Isabella?

EVELYN: Well, what he said was that you were real depressed about tomorrow and he thought you would like some company . . . Only you yourself wouldn't ask, being the way you are . . .

SARA: How thoughtful of him.

EVELYN: It should be like old times, all of us together again in this house.

SARA: Sometimes old times are best left forgotten.

EVELYN: Oh, Jesus, coffee. (*As she pours herself a cup.*) I thought that rain was never going to stop. I'm glad there was a taxi at the bus station. I don't know if I could have walked here in all this heat. It feels more like August than June. How's Miriam?

SARA: The same. She still doesn't remember anything.

EVELYN: I see old Lukas hasn't changed either. How old is he now?

SARA: I don't know, but he probably feels a lot younger than I do at the moment. I really wish I had known you were all coming.

EVELYN: Sara, are you sure this is all right with you?

SARA: Of course it is. I'm just in shock, that's all.

EVELYN: On the way here I noticed the Feed Mill's reopened. That's a good sign.

SARA: Yes. There's even been some talk about bringing back the Cannery.

EVELYN: What next? The Fish-Hatchery?

SARA: Don't make fun, Evelyn. Who knows? Maybe this town will come back to life again.

EVERLYN: I hope so, for your sake. Are any of my old friends still around, not that I had too many.

SARA: I doubt it. Pretty much everyone's gone. Everyone young that is. There's not much to keep them here anymore. But you know that . . . So, how is life in the big city?

EVELYN: Hectic. I don't know if I'll ever get used to it.

SARA: You seem to be doing okay. I still can't believe I actually have a sister who makes money writing poetry.

EVELYN: Who still has to work from nine to five as a receptionist to earn a living. In fact, I had to work today, but I thought I could use a day off from "Kleinman, Kleinman and Kleinman, Attorneys at Law."

SARA: But, you've had your name in magazines and everything. That's very impressive to say the least. Especially for somebody from VanHornesville. Here you have to die to get your name in the paper.

EVELYN: A little secret between us, most of those impressive magazines don't pay a dime. Some of them don't even give me free copies. That's how they make their money. They'll publish anything because they know then at least somebody will buy the damned things.

SARA: I can't get over how grown up you are. You look beautiful.

EVELYN: Thanks, 'cause I feel like a dog. My backside is killing me from that bus ride. And the air conditioning didn't work. I was only thankful Isabella wasn't on the same one. You know how she is, yakety, yakety, yak . . . non-stop. I just hope she behaves this weekend. And you remember to do the same.

SARA: I will treat her exactly as she treats me.

EVELYN: Maybe she's changed, Sara.

SARA: Yeah. And maybe pigs have wings.

EVELYN: I've got to get out of these clothes. These pants feel like they are permanently stuck to my rear end . . . Is my room still vacant?

SARA: Yes. I do have two new boarders, though. Next to them. (*Indicates* LUKAS.) He's the prize. At least he sleeps most of the time.

EVELYN: I'll be down in a minute. (*Exits.* SARA *stands there a moment trying to figure out what is going on. She moves to the bar and makes herself a straight scotch, drinks some, then stands looking up the stairs a moment.*) Jason! Jason!

JASON: (*Enters wearing a white shirt.*) Yes?

SARA: You're full of surprises, aren't you?

JASON: What are you talking about?

SARA: First that phone call from Edna, then Josephine says you told them they can stay here for free, and now I find out that you've invited all of my sisters here? Jason, why?

JASON: I know what Michael meant to you, Sara. I felt sure you'd want your family around to console you on the first anniversary of his death.

SARA: I'm surprised you didn't drive into the city to pick Isabella up!

JASON: Now that would have been too much. However, I am meeting her bus. It should be here any time now.

SARA: I can't believe you're doing this, Jason.

JASON: What are you so upset about? You've always wanted your family together. And now I've given you your wish. At least for a weekend.

SARA: Fine, Jason, so long as you know that after this weekend is over, so are you and I.

JASON: That's all right by me. But make certain you'll walk away with nothing.

SARA: Nothing is more than I have! Don't think it's been worth any amount living with you!

JASON: Not with me, off me.

SARA: Jason, please do not bring that woman into my home.

JASON: Are you begging me?

SARA: If that's what it takes, yes.

JASON: You sound like my whore from last night. She begged me, too.

SARA: How could I have ever married you!

JASON: Simple. I had money.

SARA: Money you and Edna suckered out of people!

JASON: There is nothing illegal about what I do, Sara.

SARA: Finding out from Jed who the bank is going to foreclose on? Going to them and buying up their property for next to nothing? That's real legal, Jason.

JASON: At least they end up with something, however little it is. Besides, there was a time you didn't mind the profits. After all, it did rebuild your house for you.

MIRIAM: (*Enters.*) I'm ready.

JASON: I'll see you when I get back, Sara. Enjoy your day. (*He exits.*)

MIRIAM: You won't forget about Miss Margolis? (*However* SARA *can only stand there, unable to talk.* MIRIAM *exits and a car is heard driving off.*)

EVELYN: (*Re-enters.*) I'm sorry. I couldn't help overhearing. When Jason called I was hoping things had gotten better between you two. (SARA *freshens her drink.*) You wrote you had stopped drinking. (SARA*'s only response is to take a long sip.*) Don't do this to yourself, Sara. Believe me. I know how hard it's been for you. Don't think I don't appreciate all you gave up to keep us together after the fire . . . I don't know if I'd be strong enough to do it now, much less at sixteen like you were.

SARA: You do what you have to.

EVELYN: Isabella didn't. I guess that's why I've always thought of you more like a mother than my sister. It's probably even why I got so rebellious towards you after a while.

SARA: Is that why you left? Why you left without so much as a word for two years?

EVELYN: We all grow up, Sara. There comes a time we all have to leave home.

SARA: I suppose so, even if I never did.

EVELYN: You never could.

SARA: I can't tell you how much I've missed you, Evelyn. When you came up for Michael's funeral last year, in a way I was hoping you would stay. I don't even have anybody to talk to anymore, now that Michael is gone. And every time I think about that bitch Isabella coming backtomourn him . . .

EVELYN: She was his wife, Sara.

SARA: She was married to him, but she was never his wife. But I guess I shouldn't even be thinking about that right now. There's so much I've got to do, what with everybody coming and all. I'm glad I at least went shopping yesterday.

EVELYN: I'll help you with dinner.

SARA: That's okay. You'll be surprised. I've even learned to become a decent cook. Don't think I wasn't on to you, the way you used to eat all those pickles just to kill the taste of my food.

EVELYN: (*Laughing.*) I didn't think you noticed.

SARA: How could I not notice? I thought you were pregnant all the time, the way you ate pickles with everything.

EVELYN: Well, I hope your cooking's better than your coffee. (*A car is heard.*)

CARMEN: (*Offstage.*) Sara! Sara! Yoo hoo! Eeee eeeep! Anybody home?

SARA: You can take the hick out of the country, but you can't take the country out of the hick! (CARMEN, *her loud, pregnant sister runs on.*)

CARMEN: Sara! Evelyn! Ay, ay, ay . . . I'm so excited I've gotta pee!

SARA: You know where the bathroom is.

CARMEN: No, I'll hold it. I want to look at the both of you.

SARA: Well, Carmen how are you?

CARMEN: Pregnant, how else?

EVELYN: So were you the last time I saw you. I hope you're not still carrying the same baby.

CARMEN: No, funny, it's not the same baby . . . or the same father for that matter.

SARA: For that matter, do any of your kids have the same father?

CARMEN: Listen, don't start, I just got through the door.

EVELYN: How many kids you got now?

CARMEN: Six.

EVELYN: Six! My God, Carmen, you're only twenty-eight years old!

CARMEN: Ahh, six is as much trouble as five and five is as much trouble as four . . . I can't help it if I'm fertile.

EVELYN: Didn't you ever hear of birth control?

CARMEN: I'm a good Catholic, what can I say? (*A car horn honks.*) *¡Pendejo!* (*She screams out the door.*) *Oye maricón,* I told you to wait a minute! (*She slams the door.*) That man, he's so impatient!

SARA: Is that father number seven?

CARMEN: He thinks he is. That's all I care about. Sara, is it okay for him to park the car in the garage?

SARA: No, tell him to park on top of one of the trees . . . Idiot, why do you think I have a garage? (*The horn honks again and* CARMEN *once more yells outside.*)

CARMEN: *Mira*, you wanna blow something? Stick a gun up your ass and blow your brains out! Just stop with the fucking horn! Park the car wherever the hell you want!

SARA: No, Evelyn, I don't know if I can take this.

EVELYN: Hey Carmen, are the kids in the car?

SARA: (*Quietly.*) For the love of God, please have left them at home.

CARMEN: Nah, I left them with my neighbor.

SARA: Thank you, God.

EVELYN: All six?

CARMEN: Why not? She's got five of her own. She leaves them with me all the time. What's eleven when you have five? (*Screams out the door again.*) Hey, dickface! Will you get inside already?

LUIS: (*Offstage.*) I'm coming! I'm coming!

CARMEN: What's the matter, you find a cow to screw out there? Stop coming and get your little ass in here!

SARA: Sometimes I think you were conceived in a toilet bowl, to have your mouth.

CARMEN: Watch it, that's your mother and father you're talking about. You don't want their spirits coming down and making you turn around in circles till you die.

EVELYN: Carmen, you will never change.

CARMEN: Why should you change when you're fabulous already? (*Indicates* LUKAS.) I see Rip Van Winkle is still alive. He must be a hundred and ten. Damn, I hope I never get that old. Who wants to look like a prune? I want to die when I'm young so everybody can say . . . "*Ay, bendito, la pobre* . . . Doesn't she look beautiful?" (LUIS, *enters with their suitcases.*)

LUIS: Hello.

CARMEN: There you are. Come here, baby. Meet my sisters, Sara and Evelyn.

LUIS: *Mucho gusto en conocerlas.*

CARMEN: Sara's married to an American so she thinks she passes. Speak English, *pollito.*

LUIS: Nice to meet you.

SARA: (*Shaking his hand.*) *El placer es mío.*

CARMEN: *Sangana.*

EVELYN: How was the drive up?

LUIS: Oh, nice, nice.

CARMEN: That's why he took the scenic route.

LUIS: She means we got a little lost.

CARMEN: A little? I thought I was going to give birth in the car and I'm not due for another three months!

LUIS: We would have gotten here fine had you kept quiet. Had you stopped trying to give me directions!

SARA: I'm sorry it took you so long.

LUIS: That's all right. I love driving.

CARMEN: Are you kidding? He loves that lousy car better than he loves me.

SARA: Maybe that's because his car doesn't have your mouth.

LUIS: (*Laughing.*) That's true.

CARMEN: I'll give you a "that's true" right across your face! Him and his car. I think I'm gonna name the baby Chevrolet.

Isabella here yet?

SARA: No, Jason went to meet her. With any luck they'll crash on the way back.

CARMEN: Sara, it's nice to be nice.

SARA: I realize it's early, but would anyone like a drink?

LUIS: I'd love one.

CARMEN: Not if you're gonna drive.

LUIS: But we're already here!

CARMEN: *Idiota*, I know we're already here. I'm not stupid. But we're going out later. We're going dancing at the Hot Potato.

SARA: I hate to tell you, Carmen, but that's been closed for years.

CARMEN: You're shitting me?

SARA: So has every place else to go dancing.

CARMEN: So what do you do for fun? Scratch your ass and count to ten?

SARA: There's a couple of places over in Starkville. With the highway it doesn't take long to get there now.

EVELYN: Anyway, Carmen, should you be dancing in your condition?

CARMEN: I'm only six months. You should see what I can do in this condition, right, lover boy?

LUIS: (*Embarrassed.*) Carmen . . .

CARMEN: Oh, it's natural, like going to the bathroom. And don't tell me you don't go to the bathroom.

LUIS: Carmen . . .

CARMEN: I live with you and believe me, you go to the bathroom. Sometimes I can't go in for an hour.

LUIS: Carmen, *por Dios* . . .

SARA: Speaking of bathrooms, didn't you say you had to use it?

CARMEN: Oh, that's right.

SARA: There's the bar, Luis. Make yourself at home while we get her upstairs and out of your way before you kill her.

Come on, Evelyn, let's see if we can do something with this one. (*The women exit upstairs.*)

LUIS: (*Muttering.*) One of these days, Carmen, pregnant or not pregnant, you're gonna find my foot down your big mouth. (*Looking over the bar.*) Hey, hey, hey. Bacardi, Dewars, Beefeaters . . . *Bueno pues . . . Aquí estoy.* (*He pours himself a straight rum as* JOSEPHINE *enters.*) Good morning.

JOSEPHINE: Yeah? Says who? (*She takes a cup of coffee and a few biscuits.*)

LUIS: You live here?

JOSEPHINE: If you can call it that. God, do I hate this place. I can't wait to move the hell out of here. Let me give you a little advice. If you're even thinking about renting a room here, don't. Anyplace would be better than this dump.

LUIS: I don't know. This looks like a nice house, if you ask me.

JOSEPHINE: Who the hell was asking? (LUKAS *has woken up and enters.*)

LUKAS: Good morning, Miss Josephine.

JOSEPHINE: Oh, gimme a break! (*She exits.*)

LUKAS: Who are you? How long have you been living here? (*Before* LUIS *can answer.*) No use telling me. I probably wouldn't remember anyway. (*Makes a cup of coffee.*) One more cup and my morning will be complete. Helps make me regular, coffee does. In one end and out the other. You know, I read in the paper this morning the price of gasoline is going down. Too bad I don't own a car. Maybe it's good that I don't, what with my mind the way it is, I'd probably forget to fill the tank and end up on the road in the middle of nowhere and die. My son sends me a check every month, did you know that? He's a lawyer, my boy Tommy is. But I can't find what I did with it. This morning I could't find my Bible or my teeth. And now suddenly here they are right in my mouth, see? (*He shows him his teeth.*) You just better hope you never get old . . . Oh, this coffee is starting to work. I'd better go use the toilet while I still remember . . .

I tell you, this coffee is better than an enema . . . Well, it was nice talking to you . . . Whoever you are. (*He exits.*)

LUIS: What's the matter in this house? Is everybody crazy? Now they've even got me talking to myself. (LUIS *a little puzzled by it all, lights up a cigarette.* ISABELLA *enters appearing quite fragile at the moment in her clothing, wet from the rain and the humidity, and hat, adorned by limp butterflies and flowers. She sets down her suitcase and she and* LUIS *stare at each other for a long moment.*)

ISABELLA: Well, what are you staring at?

LUIS: Uh . . . nothing. I just thought maybe you were somebody else.

ISABELLA: Who else could I possibly be but me?

LUIS: Nobody, lady, nobody.

ISABELLA: Would you have an extra cigarette? Mine are all wet.

LUIS: Sure. (*He gives her one and she stands there waiting for him to light it, which he does.*)

ISABELLA: Thank you.

LUIS: (*Feeling very uncomfortable with her.*) I'm Luis.

ISABELLA: Should that mean something to me?

LUIS: I don't know. Who are you?

ISABELLA: Isabella.

LUIS: Oh, you're Isabella. Your sister's talked a lot about you.

ISABELLA: I'm sure she has. Sara has always enjoyed talking about me.

LUIS: No, I meant your sister Carmen. I'm her husband.

ISABELLA: Carmen! Well, she finally got married. How nice.

LUIS: Well, we're not really married . . .

ISABELLA: No need to explain further.

LUIS: They're all upstairs. You want me to get them?

ISABELLA: (*A little too quickly.*) No, not yet. Let me pull myself together first. It's a long walk from the bus station.

LUIS: Why didn't you call a taxi?

ISABELLA: Why don't you mind your own business?

LUIS: I'm sorry.

ISABELLA: No, it is I who should apologize. That was rude, unkind and unladylike. And despite my outward appearance at the moment, I assure you I am a lady. This humidity, it's as oppressive as mid-summer in the tropics. Why anyone would choose to live there is a pure enigma. Now Paris, there you can live year round. Nothing quite cures depression like a walk along the Champs Elysee . . . Or a stroll through the sculpted gardens of the Tuilleries. And Versailles! Versailles! Nothing can match the splendor of Versailles!

LUIS: You sound like you really like it. When were you there?

ISABELLA: Quite often in my mind.

LUIS: You talk a lot, like Carmen.

ISABELLA: Do you know if Jason's here?

LUIS: Jason?

ISABELLA: Sara's husband.

LUIS: Oh no. I think she said he went to meet you.

ISABELLA: I can't imagine what could have happened to him. I even waited in the Diner nearby, but after fifteen minutes in that God-awful place, I thought I'd take my chances in the rain. (*Removes her hat.*) Jesus Christ, my hat! It's ruined. And my hair must look like a thousand pieces of string. You really must forgive my appearance. I don't usually look this dreadful.

LUIS: You look fine.

ISABELLA: Would you mind making me a drink?

LUIS: Sure. What would you like? I think they've got everything.

ISABELLA: Anything. Anything strong, that is. I'm sure going to need it. Not that I usually drink this early in the day. It's just that I'm very chilled from the rain.

LUIS: (*As he pours her a straight scotch.*) It's all right. You don't have to make excuses to me.

ISABELLA: I assure you I am not making excuses. I am merely

very wet and very tired. (*She places her hat on the suitcase.*)
No. It will never dry. My butterflies have died forever.

LUIS: Maybe not.

ISABELLA: Sir, they are dead!

LUIS: (*Stopped by her tone.*) If you say so.

ISABELLA: And I do say so! Oh, you must think me insane,
being so emphatic with you over a silly hat. And all this time
you've been nothing more than a sweetheart. A perfect
gentleman, offering conversation and drink to a lady in the
rain. It's just that the butterflies on my hat are real. I caught
them myself. And now they're dead. Well, I guess we all
have to die sometime. In fact, that's why I'm here.

LUIS: To die?

ISABELLA: To worship the memory of my dear departed
husband.

LUIS: Oh, that's right. You were married to Michael. I'm sorry.

ISABELLA: You needn't be. It was never much of a marriage.
Sara saw to that. (*Pause.*) What are you staring at?

LUIS: Was I staring? I didn't mean to.

ISABELLA: Weren't you taught any manners? Or were you
brought up like every other macho spic who feels he can
leer at a woman any time he pleases?

LUIS: Look, maybe I should call your sisters . . .

ISABELLA: No! Please don't. Not yet. I apologize. I insulted
you again. You must think me a complete lunatic. I don't
understand what's the matter with me today. I guess I'm just
more nervous than I thought. Well, who wouldn't be?
Coming back to this house where my husband died. Being
in this town to celebrate his first happy birthday in heaven.
I miss you . . . Your loving and still forgiving wife, Isabella.
That's what will be printed in the newspaper tomorrow. The
obituary column. (*She searches through her bag and takes
a pill from a vial, washing it down with scotch.*) Thank God
for valium.

LUIS: Is that okay to do?

ISABELLA: Would you mind fixing me another one of these, Luis? What was that, scotch? Funny, I normally hate the taste of scotch. It must be a rough morning. (LUIS *pours her another drink.*)

LUIS: You seem very different from your sisters.

ISABELLA: And thank God for that.

LUIS: Do you even speak Spanish?

ISABELLA: Only *cuando es necesario*. You see, unlike the others in my family, I am not proud of a heritage of ghettos and heathen ideals.

LUIS: This doesn't exactly look like a ghetto to me.

ISABELLA: Never assume.

LUIS: You know something? You're a weird lady.

ISABELLA: Is that what they've told you? I'm sure they must have. You see, my sisters all have primitive minds, pagan souls and polluted mouths. I'm sorry if I offend you, but Carmen, even Carmen who is the sweetest of them all, has about as much brains as an amoeba and about as much sophistication. God, I wish Jason was here! I hope nothing's happened to him.

LUIS: Maybe he thought the bus would be late because of the rain.

ISABELLA: May I have another cigarette, please? (*He gives her one, remembering to light it this time.*)

LUIS: Are you sure you don't want me to call your sisters? They're probably dying to see you.

ISABELLA: I doubt it.

LUIS: Don't you miss them?

ISABELLA: It's strange how one always misses one's family until they are reunited with them. It's always aggravated me the way families act at weddings and at funerals. They really are the same thing, you know. Everyone making idle promises of sooner and even happier reunions. Only to go their own way again. I wonder if any of them ever realize the next reunion may be their own funeral. I don't believe I am actually in this house again . . . (*She notices the music box.*) Would you look at this! (*She opens it and listens to the music a moment.*) This used to be mine. At least before Sara took it. She always enjoyed taking what wasn't hers. Even when we were children. But Daddy always made her give them back. He never let her keep my things. You see, I was his favorite. Well, you really couldn't blame him. I was the eldest. (JASON *enters.*)

JASON: Isabella?

ISABELLA: Jason? (*She turns and runs to him.*) Jason! I was afraid you'd forgotten all about me.

JASON: How could you think that? Have you seen your sisters yet?

ISABELLA: No, I was hoping to see you first. Luis is the only one who even knows I'm here.

LUIS: Hello. Luis Martínez, Carmen's husband.

JASON: (*Shaking hands.*) Jason Montgomery.

ISABELLA: I thought you were meeting my bus?

JASON: I tried, but I was a little late getting there. I had to drop Miriam off at school.

ISABELLA: I walked, Jason. Please don't be angry with me. I tried waiting, but those terrible people, that Diner, I couldn't . . .

JASON: Just relax, Isabella, everything's going to be all right.

ISABELLA: The walk wasn't too bad, at least after the rain stopped. And I did get a lift for a part of the way.

JASON: That's probably why I didn't see you on the road. Let me call Sara. I'm sure she can't wait to see you.

ISABELLA: Really?

JASON: (*Calling.*) Sara! Sara! (*After a moment* SARA *appears on the stairway.*) Look who's here, Sara. (*The two women stare at each other.*)

ISABELLA: (*After a pause.*) Hello, Sara.

SARA: Isabella. (*Another pause.*) How nice to see you again. (*The lights slowly dim. Blackout.*)

ACT TWO

SCENE ONE

The setting is the same, except there is now a bouquet of roses on one of the tables. It is later that evening and the moon shines bright in the night sky. JASON and HENRY are playing cards as ISABELLA, drink in hand, looks on. EVELYN is reading a book of poetry while JOSEPHINE knits and MIRIAM plays with Amanda. SARA is busying herself, collecting empty coffee cups, etc., which she places on a tray. MR. LUKAS is once again on the porch, carefully sipping his coffee.

ISABELLA: I play the winner!

HENRY: Is there any more coffee, Sara?

SARA: Sure, Henry. (*She refills his cup.*)

JASON: Looks like you still haven't recuperated from last night.

HENRY: You're telling me. I had to pull my car over to the side of the road to sleep it off, I was so drunk.

JOSEPHINE: Thanks to you, Jason.

HENRY: Don't start on him again, Josie. You didn't shut up all through dinner.

JOSEPHINE: It's the truth. Where else did you get the money from?

SARA: I heard they might be starting to hire again at the Cannery. You should check it out, Henry.

HENRY: Actually, I was meaning to stop by there today, only I got tied up with something.

JOSEPHINE: As usual.

JASON: You can blame that on me too, Josephine. I needed Henry to do me a favor in town.

JOSEPHINE: He can do me a favor right now . . . Drop dead.

ISABELLA: Don't say that, Josephine. Remember, God sometimes does grant us our wishes. (JOSEPHINE *gives her a look, then exits*).

HENRY: That woman. It's like being married to Godzilla.

Only worse.

MIRIAM: Did you see your roses, Amanda? Aren't they pretty?
(LUKAS *enters from outside*.)

SARA: More coffee, Mr. Lukas? I just put up a fresh pot.

LUKAS: No thanks, Miss Sara. Any more coffee and I'll be up
all night.

MIRIAM: An atom bomb couldn't keep you up all night.

LUKAS: I'll see you all in the morning, that's if I remember to
wake up. Goodnight, everybody.

HENRY: I'll be in to help you right after this game, Lukas. So
don't fall off to sleep till I do. (LUKAS *exits*.) I promised
I'd help him look for his check.

SARA: Poor man. Half the time his damned son forgets to send
it . . . and the other half he can't remember where he puts it.

HENRY: Well, we all know that boy Tommy never was any
good. I could never understand how somebody white as
Lukas could father a lying little nigger like that.

SARA: I will not have you use that word in this house, about
Tommy or anyone else!

HENRY: That's what he is, Sara. Spreading that filth about me
all over town . . . And here I'd let him into my home . . . Let
him play with my sons like he was a regular white boy.

ISABELLA: Nobody believed him, Henry. Not even Lukas.
You're probably the only one who even remembers it
anymore.

HENRY: That's because it was my name he was trashing to
anybody who would listen! I just thank God the good Lord
always finds ways to vindicate the innocent. Even if he does
take his sweet time in doing so. Remember, Jason, that
Fourth of July me and my boys found him down by the lake
doing things to the Minister's son so disgusting, I wouldn't
dream of doing with my own wife, I almost threw up my
dinner right there over the both of them.

ISABELLA: Please, Henry, must we be so graphic?

HENRY: Hell, we sure taught those two little sissies something about the way decent men live here in Vanhornesville, population now two fifty.

SARA: Yeah. You nearly killed them. That wasn't God's vindication, Henry. That was your revenge.

HENRY: Call it what you will, Sara. At least it rid this town of the likes of him.

SARA: That's right, Henry. Now Tommy's a big deal lawyer in New York City and you can't even pay your rent. Still, I'd much rather have you living here. You should go into politics, Henry. Not everyone is blessed with your logic.

HENRY: We were right, Sara. Even Lukas agreed. My sons and I were right to teach them fag boys a lesson, weren't we, Jason?

JASON: You always were a big man, Henry, when your sons were around. I bet those were the best times of your life.

HENRY: You're telling me they were. My boys looked up to me. I was somebody then . . . (*His voice trails off as his reality sets in.*)

ISABELLA: But why are we talking about such depressing things? All that's important right now is that my sisters and I are all home together again. And Sara, what a homecoming it was! That dinner you cooked was divine!

EVELYN: You sure meant it when you said you'd learned how. Notice? Not one pickle all through the meal.

SARA: I'm glad you enjoyed it.

ISABELLA: Enjoyed it? Why that dessert was a dream. You really should have had some, Evelyn.

EVELYN: I don't eat sweets much.

ISABELLA: That's probably how you keep your figure. Me, even looking at food is fattening.

HENRY: What are you talking about? You're as thin as a growing farm boy.

ISABELLA: Because I work at it, Henry. Except on days like today. You really shouldn't let me have had seconds of that dessert, Sara. All that fruit and brandy? I'm afraid it's gone to my head.

MIRIAM: (*Under her breath.*) I'm glad something has.

ISABELLA: What was that?

MIRIAM: Nothing. Amanda just burped.

ISABELLA: Well, it just proves that children should be seen and not heard. No matter how old they are.

SARA: I'd better start the dishes.

ISABELLA: (*Stopping her.*) Let me do that, Sara.

SARA: That's all right, Isabellla.

ISABELLA: Please. The least I can do is help you clean up.

SARA: Don't trouble yourself.

ISABELLA: But I feel so guilty. You've been in that kitchen all day preparing that delicious feast. What was it called again?

SARA: Stew. (*Walks into the kitchen.*)

ISABELLA: No wonder I can't remember the name. It tasted much more exotic than stew. It must be the way she seasoned it.

JASON: (*Putting down his cards.*) You won again, Henry.

HENRY: You know what they say? Lucky in cards, unlucky in women.

JASON: If that were true, I'd be a millionaire.

ISABELLA: I'm surprised at you, Jason. What would Sara say if she heard that? Well, Henry, it looks like it's you and me now.

HENRY: Sorry, Isabella. I'd better help Lukas while he's still awake.

ISABELLA: Afraid of losing? Well, Jason's not, are you Jason? You'll play with me, won't you?

JASON: Not right now, honey. There's something I want to look at in the paper first.

ISABELLA: The sports section, undoubtably. Isn't that just like a man? Three lovely ladies in the room and all he's interested in is the sports section.

MIRIAM: Four.

ISABELLA: Four what?

MIRIAM: (*Holding up Amanda.*) Four lovely ladies.

ISABELLA: Oh, yes . . . Four lovely ladies. (HENRY *exits as* JASON *sits reading his newspaper.* ISABELLA *is pacing somewhat distractedly, nervous and looking for someone to talk to.*) Well, Evelyn, are you still writing your little poems? You must let me read some sometime. I adore poetry.

EVELYN: (*Not really paying attention.*) Do you?

ISABELLA: You mean you don't remember? And all this time I thought you were taking after me. Well, that's life, isn't it . . . Tell me, where did you go after you left here?

EVELYN: Away.

ISABELLA: What kind of answer is that?

EVELYN: The only one you're going to get.

ISABELLA: Well, that told me, didn't it. (*Calls out.*) Sara, are you sure I can't help you in there? (*She gets no response and after a moment continues to pace, stopping at the music box.*) I'll never forget the day Michael bought this for me.

MIRIAM: He bought it for Sara, not you.

ISABELLA: He did not. It was our song.

MIRIAM: He gave it to Sara, right Amanda?

ISABELLA: That might be what she told you, but he gave it to me. I even had a record of it.

EVELYN: Does it make a difference, Isabella?

ISABELLA: Yes, it does make a difference. It makes a lot of difference. (*She looks through the records.*) We danced to it at our wedding. You remember, Jason, don't you? How Michael and I danced to it at our wedding? (*She finds the record.*) Oh, here it is. It was right in front of me all the time. (*She puts on the record, the same waltz as before.*) We danced to it at our wedding, Michael and I . . . It will be a year tomorrow, won't it . . . It does make a difference. (*The phone rings and she almost runs to answer it.*) I'll get it! (*Into phone.*) Hello? Oh, yes . . . One moment please . . . Who should I say is calling? (*After a moment she turns to* JASON.) Jason? It's for you. A woman. She wouldn't give her name.

JASON: Thank you, honey. (*He takes the receiver from her.*) Hello?

ISABELLA: For a moment I thought it might be for me. Remember how I used to get all of those calls? Why, the phone would ring off the hook, I had so many boyfriends . . .

JASON: I can't really talk right now . . .

ISABELLA: Daddy used to get so angry. It seemed like I was always on the telephone, accepting one date or another . . .

JASON: Everything looks fine. I'll have Henry drop them off to you later. Good. I'll see you soon. (*Hangs up the receiver.*)

ISABELLA: Who was that, Jason?

JASON: Nobody special. One of my business partners. (*He returns to his paper.*)

ISABELLA: All right, don't tell me if you don't want to. (JASON *continues to read.*) I don't think I'll ever get used to the idea of women in business. It's so unfeminine. (*Although* JASON *is quiet, we should get the feeling that he is not only aware of what is going on, but in a way is pleased.* ISABELLA *by now, is somewhat beside herself looking for something to do. After a pause.*) This house seems so different today. So quiet. When we were kids there was always something or other going on. This was a happy house. Remember how in the evenings Mommy and Daddy would get dressed up in their fine clothes and it would be like a party? There were always guests here then . . . and Mommy and Daddy would get up and dance . . . (*She takes the boa as she dances.*)

MIRIAM: Give that back to me!

ISABELLA: I just want it for a minute.

MIRIAM: I said, give it back to me. That's Amanda's!

ISABELLA: I'm just borrowing it.

MIRIAM: I said give it back!

ISABELLA: All right! All right! (*Flings it at her.*) Take the damned thing!

MIRIAM: (*Leaves it on the floor where it's fallen.*) Forget it. I
    don't want it now.

ISABELLA: What is wrong with you, Miriam?

MIRIAM: Amanda says to go to hell!

ISABELLA: Well, you tell Amanda . . .

EVELYN: Isabella . . .

ISABELLA: You tell Amanda she's going to end up in the
    garbage dump with all the rest of your dolls!

EVELYN: Isabella, calm down, please . . .

MIRIAM: You wouldn't dare.

ISABELLA: Oh, wouldn't I? Come here, Amanda . . .

EVELYN: Jesus Christ, Isabella, don't you feel just a little bit
    silly arguing with a damned doll?

ISABELLA: (*Pause.*) You're right. You're right, Evelyn, and
    I'm sorry. I'm sorry, Miriam, and I'm sorry, Amanda. I don't
    want to argue. I don't want to think about the bad times. I
    only want to think about the good times. I want to remember
    Mommy and Daddy dancing. How she'd put on her blue
    feathers and Daddy would ask me to dance. He liked
    dancing with me. I was the best dancer . . . Miriam, come,
    let's be friends. Dance with me.

MIRIAM: No.

ISABELLA: Forget what I said before. Dance with your big
    sister.

MIRIAM: I said no.

ISABELLA: Have it your own way. Don't have any fun . . .
    Evelyn, you want to dance with me? (EVELYN *ignores*
    her.) Jason?

JASON: I'm sorry, Isabella, did you say something?

EVELYN: Leave him alone, Isabella.

ISABELLA: Henry!

HERNY: (*Entering.*) Yes?

ISABELLA: I can't seem to find a partner. You'd like to dance
    with me, wouldn't you?

HENRY: I'm sorry, Isabella, not right now. I'm kind of busy

inside. (*He exits.*)

ISABELLA: Why won't anybody dance!

MIRIAM: Aren't you a little old to be acting so dumb?

ISABELLA: And aren't you a little old to be playing with dolls?

MIRIAM: Amanda's not a doll!

ISABELLA: No? Then what is she? She's just a bunch of rags!

EVELYN: Isabella, leave her, please.

MIRIAM: Bitch, Amanda's not a doll!

ISABELLA: You'd better watch your mouth, young lady.

MIRIAM: Oh, shut the hell up!

ISABELLA: I'll smack your little face for you!

EVELYN: For Christ's sake, will you leave her alone?

ISABELLA: You mean you approve of her talking to me like that?

EVELYN: Please, Isabella . . .

ISABELLA: Please, Isabella, what? What am I doing that's wrong? All I wanted to do was have a good time. Why did she have to start in on me? I didn't do anything wrong. I was just having fun. Is there something wrong with that?

JASON: (*After a pause.*) Miriam.

MIRIAM: Yes, Jason?

JASON: Don't you think you should apologize to your sister?

MIRIAM: No.

JASON: Not even for me?

MIRIAM: Okay, Jason, but only for you . . . I'm sorry, Isabella.

EVELYN: (*After a pause, with contempt.*) Jason, how could you?

JASON: How could I what?

ISABELLA: Leave her alone, Jason. Of course she'd side with Miriam. None of my sisters ever liked it when I had any fun. They always had to find something wrong with it. They always had to spoil my good time. I could never do anything right according to them. Daddy was the only one who ever let me have fun . . . I was his favorite.

EVELYN: I'm going for a walk.

ISABELLA: Oh, now she's upset.

EVELYN: Don't be silly.

ISABELLA: You never did like arguments.

EVELYN: Who does, Isabella?

ISABELLA: You always were such a sparrow. The moment someone even raised their voice you'd fly away and start to cry. Which was strange, considering you were such a rough child in every other way . . . climbing trees and playing baseball . . . It was hell to even get you to put on a dress . . . not that I blame you. You always were so scrawny. Your legs looked like two little toothpicks. In fact, Daddy nicknamed you Flamingo Legs. Isn't that hysterical, Jason? Flamingo Legs! Oh, she was such a tomboy it was always a shock she showed any feminine emotions. I guess that's why she became a poet. And now she's even gotten attractive!

EVELYN: You know, Isabella, you really are a bitch!

ISABELLA: What did I say? (EVELYN *starts out, but* JASON *blocks her path.*)

EVELYN: Get out of my way, Jason. Or do you want me to apologize to her, too?

JASON: That might not be such a bad idea.

EVELYN: I've got nothing to say to her, Jason, and I've got even less to say to you! (*She pushes passed him, however he grabs her.*)

JASON: Don't you turn your back on me, little girl.

EVELYN: I am not a little girl anymore! You don't scare me anymore!

JASON: Oh, don't I?

EVELYN: Get your goddamned hands off of me! (*She breaks away from him and exits.*)

ISABELLA: I don't understand what's the matter with her. I was just paying her a compliment.

MIRIAM: Amanda says why don't you go home?

ISABELLA: That's enough from you, too, young lady. Unless you want to go upstairs to bed right now. (MIRIAM *looks to* JASON *for support, however he goes back to reading his newspaper*.)

ISABELLA: You're still not going to read, are you? I swear, Jason, you are just like my father. He was the same way. Except that he would like to read to me a lot. To tell me stories . . . When we weren't having parties or the guests had gone to bed he would sit me on his lap and read to me. He wanted me to have a proper education, to know what was really going on in the world so I could face it. But you wouldn't remember that, would you, Jason? You were never allowed into this room unless it was to help serve or clean up. And half the time you weren't around to even do that. Your mother and father would have to do it for you, remember? Oh, Daddy would get so angry at you. Like the time you showed up for my birthday party all clean and dressed up in your second hand suit . . . I almost didn't recognize you without the stink of pig shit on your clothes. But still, Daddy wouldn't let you come in. He didn't want me associating with poor boys. Remember Jason, how you stood right there and told him I had invited you? Remember Jason, how he slapped you so hard in front of everybody it made your nose bleed all over your almost white shirt? Remember how you ran away crying like a baby while everybody laughed? Even Michael, who had always defended you . . . Who had worshipped your strength, couldn't help laughing. You looked so silly in your new old suit. Remember Jason? Well, do you?

JASON: (*Not looking up from his paper.*) I remember, Isabella. I remember.

ISABELLA: Jason, put down that goddamn newspaper before I burn it!

JASON: (*Meaning it.*) Stop it, Isabella.

ISABELLA: I swear it, Jason, put it down or I will . . . I swear to God, I will. (*She strikes a match and throws it at him.*) I swear it, Jason! (*She throws another match, then another.*)

JASON: Isabella!

MIRIAM: (*Screaming.*) No! No! Stop it! Stop it!

ISABELLA: Miriam . . .

MIRIAM: Mommy! Mommy!

SARA: (*Running on.*) What the hell is going on in here!

MIRIAM: Mommy! Mommy!

SARA: (*Cradling her.*) It's okay, Miriam. It's okay.

MIRIAM: Mommy . . .

ISABELLA: I was only joking, Miriam, see? Everything's all right.

MIRIAM: Mommy . . .

SARA: Shhh, honey, shh . . .

MIRIAM: Amanda's scared of fire. Amanda's scared of fire, Mommy. (HENRY *enters and watches from the archway.*)

ISABELLA: But there is no . . .

SARA: Shut up, Isabella.

MIRIAM: Mommy.

ISABELLA: Don't tell me to shut up. She's my sister too!

MIRIAM: Mommy . . .

SARA: Jason, will you get her the hell out of here!

ISABELLA: Amanda's all right, Miriam. Amanda's fine, see?

SARA: Damn you, Isabella!

ISABELLA: Everything is okay.

MIRIAM: Stop it! Stop it! (*She screams with full force.*) Stop it! (*She suddenly goes limp, crouching in the corner as she clutches Amanda.* SARA *is trying to soothe her, but* MIRIAM *is in a daze.*)

SARA: It's all right, honey. Everything's going to be all right. (MIRIAM *doesn't respond.*) God damn you, Jason, how could you let this happen? How could you let her frighten Miriam like that?

ISABELLA: It's not his fault, Sara.

SARA: You keep out of this!

JASON: It's the truth, Sara. We were just playing a little game, that's all. (SARA *continues to glare at them, almost shaking from her anger.*) You know how Miriam gets sometimes. Nobody is to blame, Sara.

ISABELLA: Forget it, Jason. She won't believe you. Lord knows she's never believed anything I've ever said.

SARA: I wonder why, Isabella? I wonder why? (*She tries to get* MIRIAM *up, however* MIRIAM *is in her own world.*)

HENRY: Let me help you, Sara. (*The two of them get* MIRIAM *on her feet and* SARA *takes her upstairs.*)

ISABELLA: Jason . . .

JASON: (*To* HENRY.) What the hell is taking you so long in there?

HENRY: Lukas went into one of his stories. I couldn't get him to stop talking.

JASON: Did you find it? (HENRY *looks at* ISABELLA *and not wanting to talk in front of her, exits onto the porch,* JASON *following.*)

ISABELLA: Jason, where are you . . . (*But he is gone. Alone,* ISABELLA *makes herself a drink and washes down another valium before sitting down quietly as the lights dim a little on the parlor, coming up full on the porch.*)

HENRY: I don't feel right about this, Jason.

JASON: I don't remember asking you for your opinion.

HENRY: But what's he gonna do for money?

JASON: That's no concern of yours.

HENRY: He's an old man, Jason. Why can't you leave him in peace?

JASON: He can rot in hell for all I care. Him and all the rest of the sanctimonious bastards in this town. Now did you find the check or not? (*After a pause* HENRY *takes the check from his pocket and hands it to* JASON *who looks it over.*)

HENRY: He asked me to drive him to church on Sunday. I told him I would.

JASON: (*Handing him back the check.*) Sign it. (*He gives him a pen and another small piece of paper.*) Here's a copy of his signature. (HENRY *stares at the check a moment.*) Sign it, Henry. It's not like it's the first time you've forged a name on something.

HENRY: What if somebody finds out, Jason?

JASON: Somebody's already found out about you, Henry. You're only lucky Jed called me before the police.

HENRY: I appreciate you paying him off, Jason. I'll get you the money. Like I will for the back rent, too.

JASON: What are friends for, Henry? Sign the check. (*After a moment*, HENRY *does*.) Consider your rent paid. (*He looks at the signature*.) You're getting real good at this. Lukas himself wouldn't know the difference. You could have made yourself some real money if only you had half a brain.

HENRY: Sometimes that streak in you runs so evil, Jason.

JASON: Spare me the morality. There's enough of that already in this house without you adding yours to it.

HENRY: I wish I could put this all behind me. Go away somewhere and start over again.

JASON: You are a pederast and an embezzler, Henry. Believe me, wherever you went you can be assured your abberations would follow. You're fifty-three years old, Henry. Unfortunately the little boys you lust after aren't looking for daddies. At least for poor ones. Or are you fool enough to believe you are bright enough to ever make enough honest money to pay for your deviation?

HENRY: I'd change, Jason. People can.

JASON: Not you, Henry. You relish the pain of humiliation. It's what you pay for. Not the sex . . . the debasement. You must have loved it the time you invited me to play with your boys. I kicked your big, ugly, naked butt so bad it was a long time before you dared stick it back up in the air again like a dog. (HENRY *can only stare at him, silently*.) Don't look at me like that, Henry. You should know by now it makes no difference to me how many young boys you want to cornhole you. Hell, get yourself plugged by bulls and horses for all I care. Just so long as you do what I say. Understood?

(*After a moment,* HENRY *nods.* JASON *takes out an envelope from his pocket.*) Now, I want you to go inside and shit, shower, and shave, or do whatever you do to make your pathetic self a little less revolting. Then I want you to take these papers back over to Edna's for me tonight. And put on some of that sweet-smelling cologne you love to bathe yourself in, as I've told her to fix you up with something special. Something untouched and pure enough to be soiled by your corruption. Something that will make you feel even less than the man you already are not. Consider it a bonus. (HENRY, *humiliated, looks at him a moment longer, then starts inside.*) Think, Henry, for once in your miserable life you will finally have the distinctiion of being first at something, even if it is being paid for by my money. You should thank me, Henry. (HENRY *stands there a moment, not looking up.*)

HENRY: (*Quietly.*) Thank you, Jason. (*He exits into the house.*)

ISABELLA: Jason? (*However,* HENRY *continues to his room.* ISABELLA *rises and walks slowly onto the porch where she stands watching* JASON *silently a moment.*) Have I been a bad girl?

JASON: No, Isabella.

ISABELLA: Then you're not angry with me?

JASON: There's nothing to be angry about. (*The sky begins to darken slightly, the winds coming from the other direction.*)

ISABELLA: Jason, I've been meaning to ask you all day, why are you wearing that terrible shirt? You know I don't like white shirts. Didn't you like the blue one I gave you?

JASON: Of course I did. It's at the laundry. I wore it yesterday.

ISABELLA: You didn't tell Sara it was from me, did you?

JASON: No.

ISABELLA: (*After a pause.*) I bought you another present, Jason. But I didn't bring it with me on purpose. This way you'll have to come visit me to get it.

JASON: You shouldn't be spending your money on me, Isabella.

I should be the one buying you things.

ISABELLA: Just your visits are presents enough. I love buying you things. Wait till you see it. No, I won't tell you what it is. I did without cigarettes for a month to be able to afford it. Jason, I almost didn't come today. I was afraid to come back to this house again.

JASON: This is your home, Isabella. Or soon it will be.

ISABELLA: I'm afraid that will be never.

JASON: Trust me. Just trust me a little longer.

ISABELLA: Don't you want to know what I bought you? It's a sweater. A blue cardigan sweater. I like the way you look in blue. Daddy used to wear blue, too.

JASON: I know. It was his favorite color.

ISABELLA: It's so good to see you, Jason. I only wish I wasn't so afraid. (JASON *sits next to her.*)

JASON: What more can I do to show you there's nothing to be afraid of anymore?

ISABELLA: (*Embraces him.*) Jason, dear Jason, I don't know what I'd do without you. I can't tell you how much I look forward to your visits. It just pains me so much when you leave. I wish you could stay with me forever. Sara doesn't love you.

JASON: Don't you think I know that?

ISABELLA: Then why won't you leave her?

JASON: Soon, Isabella, soon. Trust Daddy.

ISABELLA: (*After a pause.*) Do you still think of Michael at all? I'm surprised at how much I think about him. Except when I'm with you. I feel so good when I'm with you. I feel almost like a little girl again . . . (*She moves closer to him.*) Put your arms around me, Jason. Hold me tight. Hold me so tight that I won't feel afraid. (*He puts his arm around her.*) You're so powerful, Jason. Everything's all right when I'm with you. Hold me tighter. Hold me till I almost break.

JASON: Isabella . . .

ISABELLA: Shhh . . . Don't say another word, Daddy. Let's just sit here and watch the world go by. (*She curls up in his arms as the lights dim on the porch, coming up full on the parlor when* CARMEN *and* LUIS *are coming down the stairs, she in the lead. She is wearing a sequined maternity dress and is singing, moving as sexily as she can in her condition.*)

CARMEN: (*Singing.*) *Mi cerebro es lo último*
          Mi cintura es lo último
          Que mi cerebro es lo último (*Doing a bump and grind.*)
          Yo no quiero que me digan
          Que lo último no sirve pa' gozar
          Sabroso, no, no, no, no, no?

LUIS: No! Carmen, what am I gonna do with you?

CARMEN: Make me a drink, papito.

LUIS: *Que mucho manda.*

CARMEN: What do you expect? I'm pregnant. I can't do anything for myself.

LUIS: You're such a liar, Carmen. All you are is lazy.

CARMEN: *Wátchealo.*

LUIS: It's the truth. You've got to be one of the strongest women I know, but also one of the laziest.

CARMEN: I'm not lazy. I'm just delicate.

LUIS: Yeah, like a truck.

CARMEN: (*Laughing.*) But I'm still pretty, right?

LUIS: I just wish sometimes you wouldn't talk so much.

CARMEN: You didn't answer my question.

LUIS: Yes, you're pretty.

CARMEN: Even pregnant you find me pretty?

LUIS: To me you're the prettiest woman in the world.

CARMEN: Am I prettier than my sisters?

LUIS: Well . . .

CARMEN: I'll give you a well!

LUIS: Speaking of your sisters, what's the matter with Isabella?

CARMEN: What do you mean?

LUIS: *Esa está craquéa.* She's cracked!

CARMEN: Don't say that, Luis.

LUIS: It's the truth.

CARMEN: It might be the truth, but don't say it.

LUIS: (*Making the drinks.*) Did you call the kids today?

CARMEN: Yeah, they send you their love. They miss us already.

LUIS: Good. I miss them, too.

CARMEN: It's good they like you so much, even though you're
so ugly.

LUIS: Ugly? Me, ugly? Heh! I look like Mr. America. (*Poses,
flexing his muscles.*) Come here, feel my muscles.

CARMEN: (*Gooses him.*) That's the only muscle you've got.
(*They laugh and she hugs him.*) Luis, please don't walk out
on me like all the others.

LUIS: You know I won't.

CARMEN: (*A bit embarrassed by her honesty, yells upstairs.*)
Hey, come on everybody! Party time! Party time!

SARA: (*Entering.*) Carmen, what have you got on? You look
like a pregnant lightbulb!

CARMEN: Did you hear that, Luis? You still find me sexy, no?

LUIS: Right now, no.

CARMEN: Hmm. That's why he just tried to screw me upstairs.

LUIS: Carmen, you've got to open your mouth about everything!

CARMEN: With you, better my mouth than my legs.

LUIS: Carmen!

CARMEN: I told you, six months was the limit. Can you believe
it, Sara? This one is even hornier than me.

LUIS: *Si tú no te callas . . .*

CARMEN: It's the truth, isn't it? Tell me you're not horny? Well,
for the next few months you're gonna have to settle for . . .

LUIS: Carmen, will you shut up!

CARMEN: Don't scream at me. You want me to have a miscar-
riage?

LUIS: *Qué vida.*

CARMEN: Listen, if you don't like your life, then go. Leave.

See if I care.

SARA: Carmen . . .

CARMEN: No, if he wants to leave, let him. He wouldn't be the first one.

LUIS: What's the matter with you? Are you crazy? Did you ever stop to think if I leave, who's gonna want you with seven kids.

CARMEN: Six. I can always abort.

SARA: I need a drink.

LUIS: It's too late to abort.

CARMEN: Then I'll give them away.

LUIS: Will you shut up! Those are my kids you're talking about. I don't like that kind of talk.

SARA: If you two don't stop . . .

CARMEN: Oh, we're only joking Sara, right baby? We always fool around like this . . . (*She looks at* LUIS *who is really upset.*) Come here, baby. *¿Oye, chulín?* Come to mommy . . . (*After a moment he goes to her and she sits him on her lap, kisses him and pushes him off.*) You're too heavy. (*To* SARA.) You should move to the city, Sara. This place is like a morgue.

SARA: I like the quiet.

CARMEN: Well, that's your choice. As for me, I'd go crazy. I mean this is a nice house and everything. I wouldn't mind owning it. Just so I could sell it! Was that Miriam before? What happened?

SARA: She just starts to remember sometimes, then she just sits there in a corner holding Amanda and calling out for Mommy, like when they found her. Sometimes I think it might have been better if she had died, too.

CARMEN: Don't say that.

SARA: She's quiet now, but she'll be up half the night . . . I need some air. (*She starts out on the porch followed by* CARMEN *and* LUIS, *the lights returning to full in that area.* JASON *and* ISABELLA *are in the same position as before.*) Excuse us!

ISABELLA: (*Breaking away.*) I assure you it's not what you think.

SARA: I assure I couldn't care less.

ISABELLA: I believe I left my drink inside.

SARA: Really? I thought it was glued to your hand. (ISABELLA *ignores the remark and exits into the house where she nervously fixes herself another drink.*)

JASON: Can't you even try being polite?

SARA: I was being polite.

JASON: Sara . . .

SARA: Go to hell, Jason. You and her.

CARMEN: Listen, I came up here to visit, not to hear fights, okay? After I leave, kill each other if you want, but while I'm here, just control yourselves. The both of you.

JASON: You're right, Carmen. Forgive us.

CARMEN: Hey, come on, why don't you both come dancing with us tonight? We'll go to that place in Starkville, you said, Jason.

JASON: I'm afraid your sister and I don't dance anymore, Carmen. It gets in the way of her mourning. (*He exits into the house.*)

CARMEN: Well, I tried.

ISABELLA: Jason . . .

JASON: I'll be right back, honey. There's something I've got to take care of.

ISABELLA: Don't leave me alone, Jason.

JASON: I'll be right inside. (*He exits inside* ISABELLA *stands there alone, not knowing what to do.*)

SARA: Why did she have to come here?

CARMEN: You have to understand that she's different from us, Sara. Always has been and always will be. I kind of felt sorry for her. I don't think even Mommy and Daddy liked her too much.

SARA: What are you talking about? She was Daddy's favorite.

CARMEN: Favorite what? In a way you can't blame her for

being jealous of you. She knew they preferred you.

SARA: That's not true.

CARMEN: I lived in this house, too. Even when they died, they left the house to you. And she is the eldest.

SARA: A half burned down house. What kind of legacy is that?

CARMEN: It's more than what she got. More than any of us got.

SARA: I asked you all to stay and help rebuild it. That it would be ours. But nobody wanted it then.

CARMEN: It's not the fact that it was worth anything, but it still must have hurt her that it went to you. Anyway, I don't think she's too terrific upstairs, you know? But she's still our sister. She's still family. (*Slaps her arm.*) These fucking mosquitoes. I'll take my chances inside. (*She enters the house, followed by* LUIS. SARA *stays there a few moments, trying to decide what to do.*) Hey, Isabella? Feel like going dancing?

ISABELLA: Thank you, Carmen, but I don't think it would be proper for me today.

CARMEN: What is it with everybody? Am I the only one in this family who's got any life?

ISABELLA: Why do we have to go dancing? Why don't we all just sit down and talk?

CARMEN: Why?

ISABELLA: So we can get reacquainted. (*Pause.*) Well, somebody say something.

LUIS: (*After a pause.*) How's your hat?

ISABELLA: I'm afraid it's dead.

CARMEN: What?

ISABELLA: It's a private joke between Luis and I. I know . . . I'll start. Luis, tell me about yourself. I hardly know anything about you. I don't even know what you do for a living. You do work?

LUIS: Of course I do. I'm a mechanic.

ISABELLA: A mechanic? How exciting.

LUIS: Well, I love working with my hands. I love fixing things.

ISABELLA: I'm glad someone does. Me, I can't tell one screw from another.

SARA: (*Entering.*) I'm sure you can't.

ISABELLA: (*Ignoring the remark.*) Did you go to school for that, Luis, or did you just pick it up?

LUIS: No, I just picked it up.

CARMEN: Like he did me! (*She bursts into laughter.*) We met in a Chinese Restaurant of all places. I had taken the kids out for a combination plate. You know, for one of their birthdays. Little did I know I was gonna bring home the eggroll.

ISABELLA: Oh, Carmen, that's delicious. So, Luis, what school did you graduate from?

LUIS: I never did. You see, I had to quit.

ISABELLA: Quit?

CARMEN: (*Getting happily excited.*) But he got his equivalency diploma! One day he was drawing this little dog off a matchbook cover, you know, the kind that say "Can you draw this?" Then he noticed the high school advertised on the other side. He sent away for the courses and now he's a high school graduate! Yeah! (*She applauds and kisses him.*) The kids were so proud of him! They took him for Chinese.

ISABELLA: As well they should have. Still, it's hard for me to understand how anyone can willingly quit school.

LUIS: Sometimes you don't have a choice.

ISABELLA: There's always a choice, Luis. You just have to make the right one.

SARA: Bullshit.

CARMEN: Sara . . .

ISABELLA: That's all right, Carmen. You see, Luis, Sara's never forgiven me for going off to college after our parents died. She's always been a little jealous of me because of it.

SARA: I have never been jealous of you for that or any other reason.

ISABELLA: The hell you haven't. Because of school, because

of Daddy, because of Michael.

CARMEN: Hey, stop it already.

ISABELLA: It's the truth, Carmen.

CARMEN: I don't care if it is.

ISABELLA: She's never forgiven me for walking away from the glorious ashes our dear parents left us to live in. For wanting more out of life than a third rate boarding house in a forgotten town nobody in their right mind would come to! She doesn't understand that unlike her, I was tired of having to work out in the fields like a goddamned nigger slave with a bunch of low lifes I wouldn't so much as spit on!

SARA: No, but who you would sure sleep with fast enough.

ISABELLA: Lies, all lies! Started by you!

SARA: How many drinks have you had, Isabella? Or have you honestly deluded yourself into believing in your own virginity? With you it was always the poorer the boys, the dirtier, the better!

ISABELLA: I never slept with any of them. That's why they said those things. Because I wouldn't. Because I hated them. I hated having to be near them! And why should I have been? To make money to keep this goddamned house!

SARA: You sure wanted this goddamned house when it was making money!

ISABELLA: Who wouldn't? I would have been crazy not to! But after it stopped making money. . . . After you couldn't pay people to stay here. . . . After Daddy stopped loving me. . . . After he forced me to work with those horrible people, no! Just so he and Mommy could drink whatever money we did make?

SARA: This house had been their dream. They tried to keep it going.

ISABELLA: At our expense! Well, I had my own dreams. I at least wanted an education. I at least wanted to do something with my life!

SARA: And what have you done with it that's so great.

ISABELLA: I can at least go anywhere and not have people laugh at me. Not think I am just another dumb spic!

CARMEN: Look, stop right there! I hate that damned word.

ISABELLA: Why? Am I offending you and your husband?

CARMEN: What you're doing is making an ass of yourself! You can't offend us, Isabella, no matter how much you seem to want to, because unlike you, we're not ashamed of who we are.

ISABELLA: Some people have no shame.

CARMEN: Like you . . .

LUIS: Leave her. People like her aren't worth arguing with, you know that.

ISABELLA: Thus spake Zarathustra. Tell me, Luis, can you draw this? (*She gives him the finger.*) What other pearls of wisdom would you like to bestow upon us?

LUIS: Lady, I don't care what you think about me. All I care about is what I think about me. But if you want to know the truth, I'm sure for all your fancy words, it's a hell of a lot more than you think of yourself.

ISABELLA: And where did you get your degree in psychology? The University of Matchbook Covers? Or did you splurge on another night on the town and find it in your fortune cookie with your three dollar combination plate?

LUIS: Maybe I don't have too much money and maybe you are smarter than me, but at least I am smart enough to have a wife that loves me. A family that respects me for who I am, not for what I can give them. Children who thank God for whatever I can afford to put on the dinner table, so they don't have to go hungry like my brothers and sisters and I did when my own father walked out on us!

ISABELLA: And just how many of those grateful little children are yours, Luis?

LUIS: I consider them all mine!

ISABELLA: How admirable, considering I'm sure Carmen herself can't tell you the fathers of most of her litter.

CARMEN: At least I kept my kids, Isabella!

ISABELLA: Don't get so excited, Carmen. I really do think your children are fortunate to have Luis as their provider. At least he does provide. Which is more than I can say for dear old Daddy after a while.

CARMEN: Maybe towards the end there wasn't too much money . . .

ISABELLA: There was no money is more like it.

CARMEN: But there was always food on the table . . .

ISABELLA: Garbage is what there was! There was always enough money for liquor though. For that there was plenty! In fact, by the end they would have sold us on the God damned street for a drink! However, Carmen, you've never been too bright. Daddy could sell you anything in one of his drunken monologues.

SARA: And the only time you ever believed him was when he bought you a present.

ISABELLA: Nobody could sell me faith in place of food. Mommy, with all of her prayers, could not convince me her God would provide when I knew damned well that loaf of bread would remain one loaf and that that fish was not going to multiply! Her God! Where the hell was her God then?

SARA: Where is your God now?

ISABELLA: He is with me because, as they say, God helps those who help themselves.

SARA: And Isabella has always helped herself!

ISABELLA: You're damned right I have. It was easy for you to leave school, to work in the fields, to pick apples for the rest of your life, because you never wanted anything. The only dream you ever had was to waltz with Daddy on a merry-go-round! Waltz on a merry-go-round! Perfect! The two of you going around in circles never getting anywhere!

SARA: What I wanted was my family to stay together! My family meant something to me. Even you, Isabella. I would have done anything to keep this house. To make Mommy and Daddy's life not seem so worthless. Even force myself to love you.

ISABELLA: You never gave a damn about me.

SARA: That's why I accepted you back here after I vowed I wouldn't! That's why I took you back after you were thrown out of your wonderful college for being the cheat and the liar you are! Why I let you live here after Michael lost his property and you had nowhere else to go!

ISABELLA: It wasn't me you wanted here!

SARA: That's right, Isabella. After Mommy and Daddy died the only place I wanted you was in hell! You used them like you've used everybody your whole life. You never loved them. You didn't even cry after the fire. After they died!

ISABELLA: If they hadn't been drunk there would have been no fire! We could have all been killed!

SARA: No, Isabella, we could not all have been killed! They knew exactly what they were doing! That fire was no accident! They did it themselves. They thought it was their only way out. That we would collect the insurance money. That maybe then we would have the chance you were always complaining they denied you!

CARMEN: Oh my God, no!

SARA: Oh my God, yes! You were out with one of those boys you claim you hated. Carmen, you were God knows where. I was supposed to take Evelyn and Miriam to Sunday Mass, only Miriam wouldn't go without Amanda and when I said no, she hid from me up in the attic and so I left her here. I didn't know what they were going to do. I didn't know . . .

ISABELLA: Because none of us were home doesn't mean that it wasn't an accident.

SARA: Why do you think there was no insurance money? Or do you think I kept it all for myself like you would have! It was no accident, Isabella. They left too much evidence around! They failed even in that! I would have done anything to keep this house. Not to make their lives into a complete joke. And you, Isabella, not one tear!

ISABELLA: Because I don't enjoy carrying on in public like all the other memebers of this pathetic family, doesn't mean I didn't cry. Doesn't mean I didn't love them.

SARA: That's why you stood there throughout the whole thing, not saying anything. Not feeling anything . . .

ISABELLA: Oh, I felt something, all right. I felt relieved!

SARA: You bitch!

ISABELLA: I felt that maybe now I would finally have a chance to get out of this hell hole of a town. That maybe now I would finally have a chance at living!

SARA: And you have gotten what you deserve. A furnished room in a lousy neighborhood, sharing a bathroom in the hallway with those same people you love to condemn!

ISABELLA: That is not true!

SARA: You are just lucky you are so sick even they can't help but pity you. That is what you have gotten for your education! That is what you have gotten for your selfishness!

ISABELLA: You go to hell, spic! (*She exits quickly upstairs.*)

SARA: (*More to herself than the others.*) Damn her . . . Damn her . . . Damn her.

CARMEN: (*After a pause.*) Why didn't you tell us before about the fire?

SARA: I never wanted to tell you at all.

CARMEN: I think I'd better lie down. Suddenly I don't feel too good.

LUIS: Are you okay, Carmen? Can I get you anything?

CARMEN: No, thank you, honey. Just sit with me for a while, okay? (*As she starts up the stairs.*) I hope I can sleep tomorrow. I forgot about all those fucking birds. They're louder than the garbage trucks. What have they got to sing about so early? (*She reaches the top and turns back to* SARA.) Try and forget about all that, Sara. (SARA *can only look at her, then she and* LUIS *exit.* SARA *stands there a moment, drained by* ISABELLA. JASON *enters from in-*

side and they stare at each other a moment, then he smiles.)

SARA: Haven't you shamed me enough without bringing Isabella here?

JASON: I don't know what you're talking about, Sara.

SARA: Goddamn you, Jason, don't play games with me! (*He looks at her as if he doesn't understand a word she is saying, then pours himself a drink of Jack Daniels.*)

JASON: There's nothing like Jack Daniels on a hot humid night. (SARA *looks at him a moment longer, then exits outside and offstage. JASON takes a sip of his drink. Then calling out.*) Henry! Henry, get out here! (HENRY *enters, bathed, his hair slicked down and in what he thinks are his most flattering clothes, holding one shoe in his hand.*)

HENRY: Yes, Jason?

JASON: Aren't you ready yet?

HENRY: Sure, Jason. I was just putting on my other shoe.

JASON: Well, put it on and get going. There's something else I want you to take care of for me. (*He exits offstage.*)

HENRY: Whatever you say, Jason. (*He quickly tries to put on his shoe; however, there is a knot in the lace, which he tries to bite loose, finally managing.*)

LUKAS: (*Offstage.*) But you can't do this to me, Mr. Jason. Where can I go at this time of night? (JASON *enters half dragging* LUKAS *with one hand and carrying his suitcase in the other.*)

JASON: You should learn to pay your rent on time, Lukas. You can't stay here for free. (HENRY *watches silently, not believing what is happening.*) Drop him off in town, Henry. Anyplace you choose.

LUKAS: But you can't do this to me! I've got nowhere to go! I'll find my check tomorrow. I swear it. (JASON *stands there unmoved.*) Mr. Henry, you'll lend me the money until tomorrow, won't you?

JASON: It wouldn't do you any good, Lukas. I've already rented the room.

HENRY: (*After a pause.*) Jason . . .

JASON: Do you have something to say, Henry?

HENRY: (*Another pause.*) Come on, Lukas. Let's go. (*They start to exit.*)

LUKAS: If you find my Bible, Mr. Henry, would you save it for me, please?

JASON: And you still believe in God, old man.

LUKAS: Oh, yes, Mr. Jason . . . I have to.

JASON: It's a pity your wife died, Lukas. Not that she would have taken you back. She was just such a fine piece of ass. First one I had when I was a boy. Would that woman squeal like a pig when a real man touched her. Even a boy-man like I was. (LUKAS *raises his hand as if to strike him.*) That wouldn't be wise, Lukas.

LUKAS: Don't you respect nothing, Mr. Jason?

JASON: Get him out of here, Henry, before the old fool hurts himself. (HENRY *stands there a moment longer then exits with* LUKAS. JASON *raises his glass in a toast.*) To you, Jack Daniels. Now you, I respect. (*He drinks up as the lights fade. Blackout.*)

ACT THREE

SCENE ONE

The setting is the same. It is later that night and dark clouds are again threatening the sky as they dance before the moon, casting deep shadows over the house. ISABELLA, *the liquor and valium having taken their full effect, is half asleep on the porch in the process of removing the butterflies from her hat. They now lay scattered about her as well as does an empty liquor bottle.* MIRIAM *quietly enters the parlor from upstairs, holding Amanda. She again wears the boa and is still in somewhat of a dreamworld.*)

MIRIAM: (*Softly.*) It's still your birthday, Amanda. It's not quite twelve o'clock yet. Are you having a good time? Did you like the presents I got you? I like the house when it's quiet like this. It's like we're the only two people in the world. I know, darling . . . I don't want to go to the cemetery tomorrow either. Well, you don't have to go. I know how frightening they can be, so don't even think about it. I know. Would you like to dance? Would you like to dance with Mommy? (*She opens the music box,* ISABELLA *begins to stir.*) Oh, so you'd rather dance with Johnny. Okay, we can all dance together. (*She picks up Johnny and they dance.*) I told you you would like him, didn't I?

ISABELLA: (*Softly, still in her dreamworld.*) Michael? Michael? (MIRIAM *surprised, quickly closes the music box and hides behind a chair.* ISABELLA *enters and looks around the room a moment.*) Michael? I know you're here, Michael. (*She notices* MIRIAM.) What are you doing there?

MIRIAM: Nothing.

ISABELLA: Sara ask you to spy on me?

MIRIAM: I wasn't spying. (*She starts back upstairs.*)

ISABELLA: Miriam . . . I'm sorry about before.

MIRIAM: What about before?

ISABELLA: You know, the fire.

MIRIAM: What fire? I don't remember.

ISABELLA: But . . .

MIRIAM: I don't remember.

ISABELLA: (*After a pause.*) I didn't know it was Amanda's birthday today. You should have told me. I would have bought her a present.

MIRIAM: No, you wouldn't have. You don't like her.

ISABELLA: Of course I do. I used to have a little girl just like her.

MIRIAM: Then why do you always say mean things to her?

ISABELLA: I don't say them to be mean. Sometimes I just don't think. Like when I'm hurt or angry. I like Amanda a lot. Let me hold her.

MIRIAM: She only likes me to hold her.

ISABELLA: Of course . . . well, seeing that neither of us can sleep . . .

MIRIAM: Amanda's the one who can't sleep.

ISABELLA: Well, seeing that Amanda can't sleep, why don't we all stay up together?

MIRIAM: I don't think so.

ISABELLA: We're sisters, aren't we? Come on, you don't have to be afraid.

MIRIAM: Who said I'm afraid?

ISABELLA: Then come, sit with me. Sit with your big sister. (*After a moment* MIRIAM *does.*)

MIRIAM: What do you want to talk about?

ISABELLA: Anything. It doesn't matter. For instance, how was school today?

MIRIAM: Same as it always is. I hate school.

ISABELLA: Really? I loved it.

MIRIAM: You didn't have people laughing at you all the time. I have a lot of fights.

ISABELLA: You shouldn't. It's not nice for girls to fight.

MIRIAM: It's not nice for them to make fun of me. I want to kill them when they laugh. Sara has to go see my teacher a lot because I fight so much. Did Mommy ever have to go to school for you before she . . . before she died?

ISABELLA: Once. She went for me once. For open school week when I was in the eighth grade. I remember because she and Daddy had a huge fight the night before and she had walked out. She left and didn't come home all night. Sara doesn't remember these things too well. At least she doesn't remember them the way they happened. Well, anyway, Mommy hadn't come home and she showed up at school, her face all painted up like a clown . . . looking like a fifty-cent tramp in this feather boa . . .

MIRIAM: I like it.

ISABELLA: Where she had been the night before, who knew? But she had gotten drunk as hell. She was still drunk and I could hear the other kids laughing to themselves as she walked, or rather, stumbled, to the back of the room to take her place with the other parents. I was mortified. You could smell the liquor ten feet away. She seemed to perspire it . . . Then after a few minutes she fell asleep and started snoring. I thought I would die. There are no sounds quite so harsh as a drunken woman's grumbling and wheezing. Everybody in the room started to laugh. Even my teacher couldn't control herself. I remember running out of that room like a bat out of hell. I wanted to strangle her with this damned boa. I was never so embarrassed in my life. I never wanted to go back to school again. I didn't know how I would face anyone ever again. Sara wouldn't remember that either. All she remembers is what she wants to.

MIRIAM: Maybe she can't remember. Like me.

ISABELLA: Oh, she can remember all right. That's all she lives for, her memories.

MIRIAM: (*After a pause.*) Amanda's getting tired. She wants to try and rest now.

ISABELLA: Miriam, I really do love you. I love you better than all of my sisters. I bet I even love you more than Sara does. You're my favorite, just like I was Daddy's. You know, if you want you can come and visit me. You can stay as long as you like. You can even live with me if you want.

MIRIAM: I don't think so, Isabella.

ISABELLA: I'd put you in a different school. A new school where nobody'd laugh at you.

MIRIAM: I don't know. Sara would miss me too much.

ISABELLA: I miss you, too. Please, Miriam, think about it. Don't just say no.

MIRIAM: (*After a pause.*) Good night, Isabella.

ISABELLA: Good night. (MIRIAM *exits. ISABELLA stands there a moment, seeming lost and frightened, then goes back out on the porch. The lights begin to dim somewhat on the parlor as she stands looking down at the butterflies. She gathers them up and begins to bury them in the dirt.*) In the name of the Father and of the Son and of the Holy Ghost, Amen. Oh my God, I am heartily sorry, for having offended Thee. And I detest all my sins because of Thy just punishment . . . (*Not realizing she continues with another prayer.*) And in Jesus Christ, His only Son, our Lord who was . . . who was . . . suffered under Pontius Pilate. Died, died, died and was buried. Bless me, Father, for I have sinnned. It's been . . . Forgive me, Father, for you must forgive me. Take onto thy breast your magnificent creatures who out of selfishness I destroyed just to satisfy my vanity. Let them fly in Heaven. Free them from this miserable world. Free me from my mortal sin. I am repentant, Father. Am I forgiven? You must forgive me. I cannot be blamed. (*There is a break in the clouds and a ray of moonlight shines through highlighting* SARA *as she stands outside in the shadows of the house, listening to* ISABELLA.) I am not God the Father, the Son or the Holy Ghost. I am only human! Please, you must forgive me, for I am to be forgiven! I have waited so long for forgiveness from Daddy . . . From Michael . . . Please don't make me start waiting all over again. Please, forgive me, Father . . .

SARA: (*Softly.*) Isabella . . .

ISABELLA: (*Almost jumping at the sound of her voice.*) You frightened me.

SARA: Come inside.

ISABELLA: No, not yet. Was I talking to myself? I do that sometimes. I guess it comes from living alone. It's such a bad habit and I can't seem to lose it. Could you hear what I was saying?

SARA: No.

ISABELLA: Good. I mean, half the time I don't know what I'm saying when I talk to myself. It would seem unfair if some one else did.

SARA: Don't worry, Isabella. I couldn't hear what you said.

ISABELLA: I couldn't sleep in that room. It brought back too many memories. I kept thinking about Michael. What time are we going to the cemetery?

SARA: I figured we'd go sometime in the afternoon.

ISABELLA: I hope the rain's stopped by then. I hope the sun is out. It won't be as depressing. It was bad enough with Mommy and Daddy there and now with Michael. Sara, I really did love them, Mommy and Daddy . . .

SARA: Isabella . . .

ISABELLA: I did. I was just afraid of ending up like them. (*A pause.*) I still don't believe I am actually back in this house again. I feel like a stranger here now. Daddy always told me if anything ever happened to him or to Mommy, this house would be mine. And now I feel like a stranger. Sara, why did you have to tell him those things about me?

SARA: It wasn't me who told him, Isabella.

ISABELLA: He hated me after that, Sara. No matter what I did afterwards, he hated me. I think that's why I did certain things. To get back at him. It's the only time he even talked to me . . . to tell me I was no good. That's the only reason you got this house, Sara, and not me. He believed all those lies.

SARA: Nobody lied, Isabella. Everybody knew.

ISABELLA: Well, everybody was wrong!

SARA: How do you explain Miriam, Isabella? Another Immaculate Conception?

ISABELLA: You promised never to bring her up to me, Sara.

SARA: And you promised never to step foot again in this house.

ISABELLA: (*After a pause.*) Daddy told me I was a disgrace to him. That he wished I had never been born. Why should I have cried when he died? Disgrace . . . that's a word nobody in this family knows the meaning of. Damn it, my whole life I've been disgraced. First by them, then by you, then by

Michael . . .

SARA: Isabella . . .

ISABELLA: Mutilating himself like that, on my bed, just to disgrace me. So that I would never have a moment's peace in this town. And everybody went around saying the poor good man this and the poor good man that. While I did not hear anybody, including my own family, grieving over the poor disgraced widow!

SARA: You don't let up for a minute, do you?

ISABELLA: I told Jason I didn't want to come here. I told him you have never forgiven me, as if it is I who has to be forgiven. You're like everybody else in this town. Always ready to accuse, to point a finger. Well, look to yourself first! You're the one he was running away with! My sister and my husband! He was a disgrace! An abomination!

SARA: Michael's only disgrace was that he loved you! That no matter how cruel you and Jason were to him, he could not stop loving you!

ISABELLA: Until you turned him against me! Until he believed your lies just like Daddy had! Jason's the only one who's ever loved me, Sara. The only one who's ever truly loved me!

SARA: For a minute before, I felt sorry for you. I thought maybe I understood some of what you've been going through all of these years . . .

ISABELLA: I do not need your sympathy, thank you.

SARA: No, all you need is Jason! Well, fine. Take him. He's yours.

ISABELLA: I don't have to take him. He wants me. You're not enough of a woman for him.

SARA: That's why he tells me every time he visits you. Why he tells me about all your little gifts. Why he tells me everything you two do. Every humiliating detail of how you abase yourself to please him! Damn you, Isabella, you are less than one of the whores at Edna's to him. At least they get paid for his perversions! (*A car is heard pulling up.*)

ISABELLA: I will not listen to you, Sara! I will not let you turn me against him, the way you've turned the world against me! (*She calls out.*) Jason! Jason!

SARA: Don't bother, Isabella. He's enjoying himself too much to come to you now. Or don't you realize yet, this is all part of his plan . . . Whatever that may be? (*HENRY enters onto the porch, his clothing disheveled, his face badly bruised, his nose still bleeding somewhat. ISABELLA looks at him, trying to regain her poise.*)

ISABELLA: Why, Henry, I'm ashamed of you. A man your age coming home in this condition. It looks like you've been fighting like a common schoolboy.

HENRY: I didn't think anybody'd still be up.

ISABELLA: You were almost right. I was just about to go upstairs.

SARA: To pack, I hope. (ISABELLA *looks at her with hatred, then exits inside and upstairs.*)

HENRY: (*After a pause.*) It looks like rain again. Sometimes I wonder if it's ever gonna stop raining.

SARA: I wish it wouldn't, Henry. It's the only thing that seems to purify this place now. (*From upstairs we hear ISABELLA knocking loudly on a door.*)

ISABELLA: (*Offstage.*) Jason! Jason, open this door. I know you're awake in there. I can hear you! Jason! (SARA *stands there wishing the world would go away.* HENRY *enters the house and starts for his room, however he decides to have a drink instead. He stands there a moment, dabbing at his nose with used tissue, his back to* JOSEPHINE *who enters.*)

JOSEPHINE: I thought I heard your car pull up.

HENRY: Go back to bed, Josie.

JOSEPHINE: Henry? (*She sees his face for the first time.*) My God, Henry, what happened to you? I'll get you something for those bruises.

HENRY: I said go back to bed!

JOSEPHINE: How'd it happen, Henry? Someone come home and catch you with his wife again?

HENRY: Josie . . .

JOSEPHINE: You were with someone tonight, Henry. And last night too . . . It's no use lying to me. I can tell, Henry. I can always tell when you've been with someone else.

HENRY: Can you really blame me? My God, woman, look at your self. Do you really believe you could be mine or anyone else's idea of a future?

JOSEPHINE: (*Really hurt by this.*) Henry . . . (*After a pause.*) I couldn't get to sleep. I've been knitting you a sweater. I know how much you like new clothes. I hope the colors are all right.

HENRY: I've got to get some sleep. (*He starts off.*)

JOSEPHINE: I wish to God we had never moved here. We were so much happier before coming to this house.

HENRY: We were never happy. I just knew how to cover my disgust for you better. (*He exits inside. JOSEPHINE stands there alone, not knowing what to do with herself. Upstairs, ISABELLA begins pounding again.*)

ISABELLA: (*Offstage.*) Jason! Jason, why won't you answer me! Jason!

EVELYN: (*Offstage.*) Jesus Christ, Isabella. It's after midnight!

ISABELLA: Jason! (*SARA angrily enters the house but is stopped by the sight of JOSEPHINE, who looks at her a moment, then exits inside. EVELYN enters from upstairs carrying a note book and pen.*)

EVELYN: That woman, I'm going to shoot her. (*SARA looks at her, appearing more tired and helpless than we have ever seen her.*) Are you all right? I was looking for you when I got back.

SARA: I walked over to the park. It seems to be the only place I can even begin to think anymore.

EVELYN: You were right about everything being closed in town. I noticed even the bowling alley is gone. I couldn't believe it. It gave me a great idea for a poem though. I was up working on it when Isabella started shouting.

SARA: She is driving me crazy.

EVELYN: Just think, you'll only have to put up with her for a few more hours.

SARA: Yes, then everybody will be going home. (*Not to think about it, she gets herself a drink.*)

EVELYN: What happened at school with Miriam? You never said.

SARA: They agreed to give her another chance, after the other girl finally admitted starting the whole thing. And she hadn't broken her arm, like Miriam thought. She only bruised it.

EVELYN: That must all be so rough on you.

SARA: Evelyn, what would you think about me coming to stay with you for a while? Both Miriam and I?

EVELYN: That's the best idea I've heard in ages.

SARA: I promise we won't be in your way. I realize you must have a lot of boyfriends now and everything, you've gotten so pretty.

EVELYN: Please, Sara, not you, too. I know I'm not pretty. I know I'm not even attractive like Isabella says.

SARA: I don't know where all your complexes come from.

EVELYN: They're not complexes. They're simply truths. Ask Isabella. At least she's always been honest about that.

SARA: Get that out of your head already . . . It wouldn't be for too long. Just till I can decide what to do with this house. I know I can't stay with Jason anymore.

EVELYN: I think the worst thing about the fire is you ended up having to marry him.

SARA: I would have married him anyway. I loved him, Evelyn. I think I was in love with him all of my life. I even remember telling Isabella about him when we'd stay up late, pretending to be asleep.

EVELYN: Mistake.

SARA: You're telling me. She never left him alone after that. I think that's why she really went off to school when she did. Not to get the education she is so proud of, but because she was infuriated somebody wanted me and not her. She didn't even stay around for the wedding.

EVELYN: It's so hard even trying to understand people like her. She could have done all right for herself if she hadn't been such a jealous bitch.

SARA: I used to feel so sorry for Jason when we were kids, the way Daddy treated him. That was my one complaint with Daddy. We had so much then and Daddy used to pride himself on how little he gave them. He had good business sense is what he used to say. Even when Jason's father died and he and his mother begged Daddy to lend them the money to bury him, Daddy refused. Here the man had worked for him . . . been loyal to him for all those years, and Daddy let him be buried in a pauper's grave mixed in with bodies of strangers. I can't blame Jason for hating Daddy. He has every right to.

EVELYN: Sometimes I'm glad I don't remember him too well. Him or Mommy.

SARA: God, it's hard to believe we were ever happy, Jason and I . . . But we were, Evelyn . . . It wasn't always like this . . . Remember how he took care of us after the fire? Paid up the mortgage when the insurance company wouldn't. How he even rebuilt this house for me as a wedding present. And now I feel like I've desecrated it by having him live here. Like I've betrayed Daddy's trust in me.

EVELYN: You've already given up half of your life for this house, Sara. You can't sacrifice the rest of it too.

SARA: Why not? Daddy did.

MIRIAM: (*Offstage screaming.*) Mommy! Mommy!

SARA: Evelyn, what am I . . .

MIRIAM: (*Offstage.*) Mommy! (SARA *quickly exits upstairs. EVELYN looks after her, wishing she could do something, but not knowing what.*)

EVELYN: (*Quietly.*) Jesus . . . (*She sits down, breathing deeply, trying to release the tensions of this past day. After a few moments JASON appears on the stairway and watches her a moment.*)

JASON: (*After a pause.*) I thought you had gone to bed.

EVELYN: (*A bit startled.*) Jason. I didn't hear you come in.

JASON: Where's Sara?

EVELYN: With Miriam . . . I'm going to see if she needs any help.

JASON: I'm sure she can manage on her own. (EVELYN *starts up the stairs, but* JASON *blocks her.*)

EVELYN: Excuse me, Jason. (*He stares at her a long moment then rubs the back of his hand smoothly across the side of her face.*) What the hell do you think you're doing, Jason?

JASON: You used to like it when I touched you.

EVELYN: Never.

JASON: You sure acted like you did. (EVELYN *stands there a moment longer, then moves away downstairs.*)

EVELYN: Jason, please . . . (*She makes herself a drink. JASON follows her down, almost stalking her as he plays his game of cat and mouse.*)

JASON: What's wrong?

EVELYN: Things have changed, Jason. I've changed.

JASON: You think so? Just like that?

EVELYN: Yes, damn it, just like that!

JASON: Keep your voice down. You wouldn't want your sister to hear, now would you?

EVELYN: Stop it, Jason.

JASON: Boy, you really have changed to think you can give me orders.

EVELYN: I'm not giving you orders.

JASON: You had better not be. Now why don't you go up to your room and wait for me to come to you like before?

EVELYN: Damn you, Jason, I was just a kid. Why'd you have to fuck up my life like that?

JASON: It wasn't your life I was fucking, sweetheart. And you were more than willing to have it fucked. Besides, you were no little girl when you came up for Michael's funeral last year.

EVELYN: Hadn't Sara gone through enough? I would have done anything to keep her from knowing then. Even sleep with one of your whores while you watched, you pig bastard. I was fifteen years old, Jason. What pleasure did you get from using me like you did?

JASON: Let's say the object of my affections no longer interested me and you were around.

EVELYN: That's all people are to you. Objects.

JASON: You were more than that. You were your sister's last ally. You were all she had left.

EVELYN: And Miriam?

JASON: That's another story.

EVELYN: You forced me away from here, Jason. You forced me away from my sister. You used me and you won. Can't we just end it there?

JASON: No. I have not finished using you. Nothing ends until I am good and ready to have it end.

EVELYN: Is that what happened to Michael? Did he try and change your ending, too? Jason, I don't know what you could have done to make him kill himself like that, but not me. I am not about to die to satisfy you! (SARA *appears at the top of the stairs.*)

JASON: Michael killed himself because Sara turned her back on him the way she had on me! He believed her lies the same way I had believed them! He never realized she could never leave this house. That this monument to cruelty built by your father had devoured her as it had him! Well, they both got what they deserved. Michael, his death and your sister, her loneliness!

SARA: You distort the truth with such ease, Jason, till it's become as perverse as your lovemaking! Michael killed himself because he was no match for you and Isabella, that's why, Jason. It killed him watching the two of you together . . . seeing you go off with her, knowing damned well what was going on. You did nothing to hide it. In fact, you enjoyed making him feel weak, making him feel less than a man. The both of you did! Isabella wouldn't so much as touch him after they moved here. She would tell him how much she wanted you. And you, Jason, you let her believe it! What I am to blame for is loving you enough not to try and stop you before I did. For wanting you enough to suffer your abuses. For being guilty enough for my father to believe you had a right to your atrocities! But Michael had no part in it, Jason. Why should he be made another of your victims?

JASON: All you have ever loved is this house. Like your father, all you have ever cared about is this damned house. And just like he lost everything, Sara, so now have you.

SARA: What are you talking about? Jason, what are you talking about?

JASON: It's gone! I sold it! Your precious house is gone, like everything else of yours!

SARA: (*Hitting him with all of her might as she screams.*) No!

JASON: (*Laughing.*) I signed it over tonight. Henry was kind enough to bring over the papers. Edna and her girls will be moving in at the end of the month.

EVELYN: You bastard.

JASON: That's why I wanted all of your sisters here. To take one last look at your house. At your family. To see what you've become.

SARA: Jason, I am begging you . . . I will crawl on my hands and knees if that's what you want. I will humiliate myself more than I already have, only Jason, please . . .

JASON: It's too late, Sara. Besides, I can't think of a more fitting end for this place . . . Or for your family.

SARA: You are so sick!

JASON: No, Sara, I am merely paying you back for all of those years I was not allowed in here. For all the degradation my family and I were forced to suffer. For being the son of a white trash unworthy of burial. The son of the woman your drunken father would come in and fuck like a mule till she bled from his wounds. The scum who wasn't good enough for that bastard's daughters. And now it's you who aren't good enough to be my whores! (*From upstairs we hear a commotion.*)

CARMEN: (*Offstage.*) Leave her alone, Isabella! Goddamn it, leave her alone! She doesn't want to go with you.

ISABELLA: (*Offstage.*) You keep out of this!

MIRIAM: (*Offstage.*) Let go of me! Let go! (*She runs down the stairs to* SARA.) Sara! Sara! (ISABELLA *enters, followed by* CARMEN *and* LUIS.)

CARMEN: (*Grabbing* ISABELLA.) What the hell's the matter with you!

ISABELLA: Get your hands off of me!

SARA: Isabella!

CARMEN: Don't start with me!

ISABELLA: You're no better than they are! All you're good for is to be screwed by any dirty little spic that'll have you!

CARMEN: (*Going after her.*) I'll slap your fucking . . .

LUIS: (*Stopping her.*) Carmen, be careful . . . leave her.

MIRIAM: Get her away from me!

SARA: Damn you, Isabella, what the hell do you think you're doing now!

ISABELLA: Jason? Jason, take me home. The hell with the cemetery! Take me and my daughter home right now!

MIRIAM: I am not your daughter!

ISABELLA: You're the one who invited me here, Jason, you can take me home! It's not my fault I'm being thrown out of here again!

MIRIAM: Make her stop it, Jason!

SARA: Isabella . . .

ISABELLA: Don't touch me!

SARA: Will you listen to me, goddamn it!

ISABELLA: No! Why should I? So you can tell me more lies? You've always hated me. You've always been jealous of me. Jason's the only one who's ever loved me. Tell her, Jason . . . tell her . . .

SARA: Yes, Jason, why don't you tell me how much you love her.

ISABELLA: He does . . . tell her, Jason, or are you going to let her make a fool out of me. Or are you afraid to tell her? Are you a coward, Jason? Are you still a coward, Jason, like you were with my Daddy? Are you going to cry and run away like when daddy slapped you? Are you? Are you going to run away crying while she makes a fool out of me?

JASON: You are a fool! You are all fools!

ISABELLA: Jason . . . (*After a moment she holds him.*) Oh my God, Jason, look at us. They even have us going at each other's throats. Oh, Jason, hold me. Just look at what they've done to us. They've made a fool out of me and a coward out of you.

CARMEN: *¡Está más loca que el carajo!*

ISABELLA: (*Charges towards her, about to strike.*) I am not crazy, you spic whore!

SARA: Damn you, Isabella . . .

CARMEN: (*Grabbing her hand.*) Watch it, Isabella. I hit back.

ISABELLA: (*Breaking free.*) Of course you do! What else would you expect from *una desgraciada, puerca sucia! Coño, me cago en ti,* Carmen! *Me cago en este pendejo! Y me cago en tus hijos!* I shit on you all!

LUIS: (*Grabbing her.*) Isabella!

MIRIAM: Make her stop it! Make her stop!

ISABELLA: *Y tú, maricón, ¿qué pasa?* You want to prove what a man you are? You want to hit me, too?

EVELYN: If he doesn't, I do!

ISABELLA: I bet you're like every other filthy spic who likes to go around beating up ladies!

CARMEN: You are not a lady, Isabella! You are not a woman, Isabella! I don't know what the hell you are! I don't think they've discovered the disease yet!

ISABELLA: Do something, Jason! Goddamn you, I said do something! (*She slaps him.*) Do something! (*She slaps him again.*) Do something! (*Another slap.* JASON *grabs her and flings her away.*)

JASON: You crazy bitch!

ISABELLA: (*Stunned.*) Jason . . .

MIRIAM: (*Who is in a corner, clutching Amanda.*) Mommy, Mommy . . .

SARA: I have had enough of you, Isabella. I want you out of this house now! Right now! I don't care where you go! Just get the hell out of this house right now!

ISABELLA: No! This is not your house. This is my husband's house.

SARA: Jason is not your husband, Isabella, as much as you would like him to be!

ISABELLA: Jason, am I to be made a fool of again? Am I?

SARA: He is not your husband now, nor will he ever be!

MIRIAM: Mommy . . .

ISABELLA: No. He is my husband. He loves me.

SARA: He doesn't love anybody, Isabella!

ISABELLA: You're lying. She's lying . . . Jason? Jason? Tell me she's lying. You're lying. Just like you lied to Daddy.

MIRIAM: Mommy, make her stop, please.

SARA: Isabella, I told you to get out of here.

ISABELLA: This is my house! It is my husband's house!

SARA: No, Isabella, it is not your house. It is not my house. Jason sold it!

CARMEN: What?

ISABELLA: You're lying . . . Jason make her stop lying . . .

SARA: Jason's the one who's been lying to you, Isabella.

ISABELLA: No, he loves me. My husband loves me.

JASON: You disgust me, Isabella.

ISABELLA: No! (*She looks at him helplessly, snapping into a former reality and sees her father standing there in his place.*) Tell them you love me . . . tell them . . . tell them you love me, Daddy. You love me . . . tell Mommy you love me best. Tell her, Daddy . . .

JASON: (*Assuming the role.*) You're a disgrace, Isabella. A disgrace to yourself and this family.

CARMEN: (*Softly.*) What are you doing, Jason?

MIRIAM: Mommy . . .

ISABELLA: Please, Daddy, please, please let me go back to school. I'll be a good girl, Daddy. I promise. Only please don't make me go back to work with those terrible people. Please, Daddy, tell Mommy I don't have to anymore. Please, Daddy, please . . .

JASON: You belong with them, Isabella. You belong in the dirt with the rest of the garbage who laugh in my face now because of you.

EVELYN: Stop it, Jason!

ISABELLA: Don't say that, Daddy. Please don't say that. Those are all lies. I never slept with any of them . . .

SARA: Isabella . . .

ISABELLA: (*Trying to embrace him.*) Hold me, Daddy. Hold me. You love me, Daddy. Why won't you hold me? I'm your favorite. You love me, Daddy. You love me.

JASON: You're filth, Isabella. You're less than filth. I should sell you to Edna!

ISABELLA: (*With the rage of a wounded animal.*) Daddy!

MIRIAM: (*Screaming.*) Stop it! Stop it! No, Isabella, don't! Don't do it, please! Please, Mommy, Amanda's scared of fire! Amanda's scared of fire!

SARA: Miriam? What are you saying, Miriam?

MIRIAM: Tell her you love her, Daddy! Tell her you love her! No, no! Isabella, no! They can't get out! They can't get out!

ISABELLA: Miriam!

MIRIAM: Please! Mommy, Mommy, please, Isabella . . . They can't get out . . . Isabella, no . . . Amanda's scared of fire. She's scared of fire . . . Isabella, please . . . I'm scared of fire . . . Mommy, Mommy, I'm scared of fire . . . I'm scared of fire, Mommy . . .

SARA: Oh my God, no!

ISABELLA: Shut up! She's lying! Shut up! Shut up! She doesn't know what she's saying . . . she's crazy! She's crazy! Stop lying!

SARA: Oh my God, oh my God, oh my God, oh my God, oh my God!

ISABELLA: Jason, make them stop lying! Jason! Destroy her, Jason! Destroy her! (JASON *bursts into laughter.*) Dance with me, Daddy . . . you love me . . . I'm the best dancer . . . (*She opens the music box.*) You love me, Daddy. My daddy loves me. I'm his favorite . . . (*She closes the box.*) I don't want to dance anymore. I don't want to dance anymore, Daddy. Please, Daddy, make the music stop. I'll be a good girl, Daddy, I'll be a good girl.

SARA: You knew all along, didn't you, Jason? Didn't you! (*The sound of the music box fades in softly.*)

ISABELLA: Make the music stop, Daddy. Make the music stop.

SARA: There is no music anymore, Isabella . . . It's ended . . . For all of us.

ISABELLA: Stop it, please, Daddy. You hear me, Daddy? Make the music stop. Make the music stop. Daddy? Daddy! (*A quick burst of thunder and lightning erupt in the sky. Blackout. The music continues a moment longer, then dies.*)

Women Without Men

by

Edward Gallardo

Dedicated to José Machado,
whose idea it was for me to write this play . . .

To my mother, Grace,
who recently lost her private war and
Anne Halitcher Taub who is currently fighting hers.

And to all the other women without men
who lived through an insane period of history
when the world had gone crazy for bloodshed.

Special thanks to BMI, Arlene Caruso, Andrés Castro, Oscar Ciccone, John Flaxman, Silvana Gallardo, Yolanda Gallardo, Brad McClelland, Joan Gallardo, Gail Merrifield, the New York Shakespeare Festival, the New York Public Library, María Norman, Joseph Papp, Iraida Polanco, Antonia Rey, Ana Rodríguez, Bruce Taub, Cecilia Vega, and the Members of the West Side Repertory Theatre for their help and support during this creation.

Characters:

DOÑA ORQUIDEA JUVENTUD: an uncompromising, domineering woman in her forties. She dresses totally in black and wears little make-up or jewelry, save for a whistle around her neck and a gold cross and wristwatch. As fanatic about the war as she is about her Catholicism and her prejudices, she has a quick wit when it comes to criticizing other people, a trait she seems born to do. She shows little mercy to, or rather especially to her daughter, Soledad.

SOLEDAD RAMIREZ: is twenty-eight years old and darker complexioned than her mother, although she wears make-up that is a few shades too light, creating a somewhat mask-like effect. She feels the war is her rival and trapped by her fate, which in a sense is true as Orquídea now lives with her. Though at times she can be dominated by her mother, there is also a rebellious side to her nature, stemming from years of resentment.

LILLIAN PACHECO: is also twenty-eight years old. She is overweight and self-conscious, though you'd never know it to hear her talk. She is angry and covers it with too many jokes and too many drinks; however, when she does attack she can be as vicious as a rabid dog.

TESSIE MINERO: is Lillian's roommate. She is a sweet, nervous, not too bright Argentinian woman in her early twenties. Although she is a war widow, she seems quite innocent to the ways of life. She is proud to be an American but has seen too many movies and so often her speech is colored accordingly.

CARLOTTA LACUBE: a thirty-seven-year-old dark Cuban woman with a penchant for hats. She is unmarried and seems to like it that way, although she has a strong sense of family. She is easygoing and tries to be everybody's friend; however, sometimes her temper gets the better of her. She believes very much in spiritualism but doesn't allow it to rule her life.

RAMONITA PAGAN: is Carlotta's niece. A woman in her late twenties. She is more tailored than the others and her make-up more simple, yet there is something about her that makes her appear quite womanly.

ACT ONE

SCENE ONE

In front of three large gated windows, their green shades raised halfway, four old Singer sewing machines are placed two in a row, representing the Sample Department of the Betty Blouse Factory, a dilapidated sweatshop in Manhattan's Garment District.

It is July, 1944, and on the cracked, water-stained, once white walls hang a white Civil Defense helmet, a photo of Franklin Delano Roosevelt, a sign reading "Buy War Bonds" and other wartime paraphernalia.

On another wall is a mirror which has a mixture of photos and magazine cut outs of actors and actresses of the time taped next to it, including a nice glossy photo of Marlene Dietrich.

USL is an ironing board and a clothesrack where the completed blouses are hung. Behind them is the door leading to the hallway and the outside world.

USR, a table used to cut patterns is diagonally placed, allowing its user to oversee the goings on in the room. Behind it is a water cooler which the women periodically drink from as well as bolts of different colored fabric which lean against the wall.

As the factory will be transformed into the employee's various apartments, the furnishings should be kept to a minimum to allow for maximum mobility; however, without sacrificing either the reality of the factory or the period of time in which the play takes place.

NOTE: *There is a lot of music in the play which either accents, comments, contradicts, or is itself part of the scene. I have included what I feel are the proper choices, of course with the agreement of the composers and artists mentioned.*

In the darkness the sound of Xavier Cugat's version of "Rum and Coca Cola"

ORQUIDEA, *the supervisor, stands at the table cutting out a pattern using scissors and a straight-edged razor.* SOLEDAD *sits sewing at one of the machines.* LILLIAN *is busy at her machine, sewing the pieces of a blouse together.* TESSIE *is at another machine.* CARLOTTA *is at the ironing board pressing the completed blouses. As the music fades.*

LILLIAN: I wish I was home right now sipping a nice tall rum and Coca Cola.

CARLOTTA: I wish I was anywhere right now sipping a nice tall rum and Coca Cola.

ORQUIDEA: Isn't it a bit early for you ladies? It's not even eleven o'clock in the morning.

SOLEDAD: I'm just glad tomorrow's Saturday so I can sleep late.

TESSIE: That goes double for me.

CARLOTTA: Me triple. I only hope I meet somebody tonight at La Conga who wants to join me.

LILLIAN: Are you still going there?

CARLOTTA: Where's better?

LILLIAN: The Palladium, sweetheart, that's where.

SOLEDAD: The Palladium? What's that?

LILLIAN: Only the hottest nightspot in New York. It used to be called the such and such Dance Studio or something.

TESSIE: Alma.

LILLIAN: What, sugar?

TESSIE: No. Alma Dance Studio. That's what it was called.

LILLIAN: Oh, that's right. And let me tell you, that place is jumping. This weekend they've even got Machito and his Afro-Cubans playing.

CARLOTTA: Machito? I love Machito!

ORQUIDEA: You love anything Cuban. Especially if it's African, too.

TESSIE: Why don't you come tonight? Lillie and I are going.

ORQUIDEA: She can't. She's got to be up very early in the morning to help out with me down at the Red Cross.

SOLEDAD: Tomorrow?

ORQUIDEA: What do you think, on Saturday the bandages get up and roll themselves?

SOLEDAD: I just wish you would have asked me, Mama. I might have had other plans.

ORQUIDEA: Armando's overseas . . . Your daughter's off at camp . . . So what other plans could you possibly have?

SOLEDAD: I've already been there three times this week, Mama. I wanted to have tomorrow to myself. To just be alone for once.

ORQUIDEA: You may know soon enough what it's like to be alone altogether and, believe me, then you'll thank me for showing you how to fill up your time . . . Other plans. My God, I'm getting married next week. Exactly eight days from today. Eight days! What could be more important than that? But still, do you see even that stopping me from trying to help? From trying to do what's right for my country? And not just you, but all of you. Instead of wasting so much time thinking about dancing . . . thinking about having fun. What you should be thinking about is giving up your time like I do. There is a war on, you know?

LILLIAN: Don't make it sound like you're the only one who volunteers, Doña Orquídea. We all do our share.

ORQUIDEA: Serving coffee and tea down at the U.S.O. is doing something? Going to their dances you think is doing something?

TESSIE: We don't only serve coffee and tea. We serve cakes and little sandwiches, too.

LILLIAN: And believe it or not, dancing with the boys sure helps pick up their morale. (*Aside to the others.*) I know the cute ones sure help pick up mine. (*The women laugh amongst themselves.*)

ORQUIDEA: Yes? Well, while you're out dancing with your Doughboys . . .

LILLIAN: They aren't Doughboys anymore. That was the last war.

ORQUIDEA: Doughboys, G.I.'s, whatever. While you're out dancing with your cutie pies, your husbands could be bleeding to death and in need of the bandages you could have rolled.

LILLIAN: You're right, Doña Orquídea. (*Again to the others.*) The next time I write to Manolo, I'll remember to include a box of bandaids.

ORQUIDEA: You swear your husbands are all coming home in one piece. That they're all coming home exactly like they left. W

ell, let me tell you, be glad if any of them come home at all.

TESSIE: Don't say that, Doña Orquídea. Of course their husbands will all come home.

ORQUIDEA: Like yours did? (TESSIE *looks at her silently, then resumes her work.*)

CARLOTTA: Listen, Doña Orquídea, since it's so important to you, I'll take Soledad's place tomorrow.

ORQUIDEA: Don't bother. Anyway, you don't even have a husband.

LILLIAN: *La mato!*

CARLOTTA: Neither do you.

ORQUIDEA: For the moment. But my first husband . . . my Lieutenant Mallory did die in the Great One. Maybe the wars are different, but the pain of death doesn't change. Nor does the loneliness of its suffering.

CARLOTTA: (*To the others.*) Fine. While she's suffering, I'll just go to the Roxy like I planned.

LILLIAN: Isn't that a little fancy for you?

CARLOTTA: What can I tell you? I'm a fancy lady. Besides, they're showing a new Errol Flynn picture.

TESSIE: Errol Flynn? Golly, I love him even more than Fred

and Ginger. He can put his boots under my bed any time.

CARLOTTA: You can keep his boots. Just send the rest of him to me. (*She hisses and trembles sexually a moment, as if she can feel his spirit, which causes the others to laugh, except for* ORQUIDEA.)

ORQUIDEA: (*Under her breath.*) *Bruja Cubana.*

TESSIE: Mind if I go with you?

CARLOTTA: Sure, why not?

SOLEDAD: Because she'll embarrass you, that's why not. It's a real tearjerker.

ORQUIDEA: And just how would you know that? (SOLEDAD *remains silent.*) Is that where you snuck off to last night? To the movies? (SOLEDAD*'s only response is to get a drink of water.*) When will you learn it isn't proper for a woman to go by herself!

SOLEDAD: I wasn't by myself. I took Victoria and the kids with me.

LILLIAN: (*Under her breath.*) Oh, oh.

ORQUIDEA: Victoria? (*She goes to* SOLEDAD.) You enjoy humiliating me, don't you? You stay up nights thinking of ways to disgrace me more than you already have, don't you? How many times must I tell you not to see that woman? Not to have anything to do with her?

SOLEDAD: She's Armando's sister, Mama. That does make her part of this family.

ORQUIDEA: *Esa desgraciada no es familia mía.* Even Armando has sense enough not to want her around. (*She moves back to her place.*)

LILLIAN: You're right about the movies, Doña Orquídea. The last time I went by myself I had to change my seat three times.

CARLOTTA: Yeah. Finally she sat down next to somebody who didn't mind her groping him.

ORQUIDEA: (*Turning her anger towards* CARLOTTA.) Honestly, Carlota, don't you think women our age should be a little more demure?

CARLOTTA: What are you talking about, our age? I'm only thirty-seven!

ORQUIDEA: Really? So am I.

CARLOTTA: *Caramba*, Orquídea! Soledad's twenty-eight! How can you stand there and tell me you're only thirty-seven?

ORQUIDEA: The same way you can tell me you are. Besides, I married young.

CARLOTTA: Well, maybe in Puerto Rico that's marrying young, but in Cuba that's child molesting! (SOLEDAD *accidentally pricks herself with the needle.*)

SOLEDAD: *¡Coño carajo!*

ORQUIDEA: Must you use that language?

SOLEDAD: I'm sorry, Mama. The needle went through my nail.

ORQUIDEA: If you paid more attention to your job, accidents like that wouldn't always happen to you. To all of you.

LILLIAN: Did it get your finger?

SOLEDAD: No, almost. (*As* LILLIAN *is about to turn away.*) Pssst. (*She whispers to her.*) I was thinking maybe you girls could come over tomorrow. You know, just sit around and do nothing for a change.

LILLIAN: What about General Eisenhower?

SOLEDAD: You heard her. She'll be at the Red Cross. Pass it on. (LILLIAN *nods and whispers the message to* TESSIE *who in turn saunters over to* CARLOTTA *and whispers to her, all seemingly unnoticed by* ORQUIDEA. *As* TESSIE *moves back to her machine.*)

ORQUIDEA: If you ladies wanted to talk about me, you should have just asked me to leave the room.

SOLEDAD: Nobody's talking about you, Mama.

ORQUIDEA: Well, you're all free to say about me what you like. All I care is that God Almighty knows what kind of a lady Orquídea Juventud is. And believe me, He knows what kind of Jezebels some of the rest of you are, too.

TESSIE: Orquídea Juventud. That's such a swell name. Youthful Orchid. It's so . . . Youthful! (RAMONITA *enters a little out of breath.*)

RAMONITA: I see the elevator's still not working.

ORQUIDEA: That's not the only thing not working today. It's about time you got here.

RAMONITA: Didn't my aunt tell you I'd be a little late?

CARLOTTA: Yes, I told her.

ORQUIDEA: 8:15 is a little late. 11:05 you might as well have stayed home.

RAMONITA: What could I do? I had to stop off at the V.A.

ORQUIDEA: Well, don't expect the company to pay for it. You should take care of your personal business on your personal time.

RAMONITA: (*As she sits down to work.*) Sometimes I'd swear she was Betty Blouse herself.

ORQUIDEA: (*Who has overheard.*) No, I'm not Betty Blouse herself, but I am the supervisor.

LILLIAN: (*Under her breath.*) Only of Sample Department.

ORQUIDEA: Anybody who doesn't like how I run things is free to transfer. In fact I heard Tokyo Rose down the hall has an opening in buttons.

SOLEDAD: Don't say that about Mrs. Chin. She's in the same boat we all are. She's Chinese, not Japanese.

ORQUIDEA: That's just what she tells people.

TESSIE: (*On the verge of tears.*) To heck with the Japs! They're the ones that got Skippy!

LILLIAN: Please don't start the waterworks flowing. I get enough of them from you at home.

TESSIE: I'm not crying. Do you see me crying? (*She sniffles them back.*)

ORQUIDEA: Don't worry, Tessie. God will have his retribution on those murderers. As surely as I am standing here, He will open up the ground beneath their feet and swallow them up into the pit of fire He calls Hell.

CARLOTTA: Right now I feel like I'm the one in Hell. It's so hot in here! How do they expect us to work?

LILLIAN: Work? I can hardly breathe! Look at me. Im sweating buckets!

RAMONITA: If we had a union we'd at least have somebody to complain to.

LILLIAN: But no jobs to complain about. You know what Betty said . . . Anyway, I worked a union shop once. It was the same crapola as here. Only there I paid dues for my crummy thirteen and change.

ORQUIDEA: Talk, talk, talk, talk! It's a pity you women aren't paid by the word instead of by the week. You'd make a lot more money.

RAMONITA: (*After a pause.*) I don't believe my morning. And to top things off the train was late again, so when it finally came it was crowded with three thousand screaming women with beach chairs on their way to Coney Island. You would think for your nickel you'd at least get a seat. You don't know how lucky you are you can walk to work.

SOLEDAD: Could they tell you anything more about Ralfie?

RAMONITA: Just that he's still missing in action. I never thought I could hate three words as much as those.

LILLIAN: I've gotten used to them by now. Reminds me of my love life. Even before the war.

CARLOTTA: That's not what I've heard.

LILLIAN: And just what have you heard? And from whom?

CARLOTTA: From the spirits, that's whom. In fact they keep me up at night talking about you.

LILLIAN: Oh, go sit on a candle.

ORQUIDEA: I want to hear machines, ladies, not your filth.

CARLOTTA: I'm sorry, Lillie. I was only joking. Don't be so touchy. (*To herself.*) *Qué sensitiva, coño* . . .

SOLEDAD: Don't worry, Ramonita. Ralfie's gonna be okay.

RAMONITA: That's what I keep telling myself, yet every time there's a knock on the door I almost pass out. I keep expecting it to be Western Union to tell me he's dead.

SOLEDAD: I know what you mean.

LILLIAN: We all do.

ORQUIDEA: Some people should be more worried the knock on the door will be their husband's.

LILLIAN: Is that supposed to mean me?

ORQUIDEA: Did I say it did?

LILLIAN: Listen, Doña Orquídea, just because I like to go out and have a good time, doesn't necessarily mean I like to go out and have a good time.

ORQUIDEA: As the Bible says, "Whoever looketh on a woman to lust after," or a man as the case may be, "Hath already committed adultery in his heart."

LILLIAN: (*Quietly, to the others.*) There should be an eleventh Commandment. "Thous shalt not be a bitch."

TESSIE: Ooh, did anybody see the paper today. I was flabbergasted. A doctor right around the corner from here was arrested for doing abortions.

RAMONITA: Yeah, I read that too. The creep did such a hatchet job, some girl hemoraged on her way home. That's how they caught him.

TESSIE: It's a shame she didn't know about the rubbers, right Lillie?

ORQUIDEA: In my day a woman waited until she got married to have sex. There was no need for abortions.

CARLOTTA: Speaking of weddings, Doña Orquídea, have you finished our bridesmaid dresses yet?

ORQUIDEA: Just about.

TESSIE: I can't wait to see them. I'm so excited! I've never been a matron of honor before.

ORQUIDEA: I tell you, I'd forgotten how much trouble putting together a wedding can be. Especially these days. At least the last time I had people around to help me. People who cared.

TESSIE: You silly goose. Of course we all care.

158

ORQUIDEA: (*Looking at* SOLEDAD.) I wasn't talking about you, Tessie.

SOLEDAD: We all know who you mean, Mama.

TESSIE: Oh . . . Well look on the sunny side, Doña Orquídea. Like your honeymoon for instance.

ORQUIDEA: With the world the way it is, who's got time for a honeymoon?

TESSIE: But that's the best part! Skippy and I went to Niagara Falls.

RAMONITA: Isn't that where we all went?

LILLIAN: Not me. I spent two glorious weeks in St. Joseph's Hospital, the Bahamas.

TESSIE: Oh, baloney sandwiches.

LILLIAN: It's true. The second day we were there Clutzola here tripped on the stairs in the hotel. Made one heck of an entrance into the lobby! Still, Manolo enjoyed it. They gave him the room for free.

SOLEDAD: I never had a honeymoon.

ORQUIDEA: Be glad you had a wedding.

SOLEDAD: If you can call it that.

TESSIE: Sometimes I think about maybe getting married again, but I don't know . . .

ORQUIDEA: What else are you gonna do? Spend the rest of your life alone?

SOLEDAD: Maybe that's not so bad, after all.

ORQUIDEA: If God wanted us to be alone, Adam would have another rib and Noah would have built a canoe. Believe me, Tessie, you've got to face life. Bury the past, no matter how comforting it might seem. If not, it will only destroy whatever future there might be for you.

TESSIE: But at least you're remarrying the same man as before. That's different. Now when I even look at a fella, I kind of feel like I'm cheating on Skippy's memory.

ORQUIDEA: I felt that way too for a long time after my Lieutenant died . . . Then after my separation from Don

Felipe. Once you've loved somebody it's not so easy to replace them. To give yourself to someone else. That's why I thank God everyday for returning Don Felipe back to me. For allowing us this second chance at happiness. That after fourteen years we will finally be rid of the sin we committed by getting divorced in the first place. (*Suddenly an air raid siren blasts and* ORQUIDEA *immediately blows her whistle.*)

CARLOTTA: The Air Raid Warden strikes again!

LILLIAN: There goes our lunch hour.

ORQUIDEA: All right, ladies, we all know what to do! (*She dons the white helmet and begins pulling down the window shades as the women unenthusiastically form a line.*)

RAMONITA: Damn it, just when I was getting started.

ORQUIDEA: Come on, ladies, look alive! Let's show them all what soldiers we can be!

CARLOTTA: Doña Orquídea, don't you think you're a bit much? We're only going to the basement, not into Nazi Germany!

ORQUIDEA: Whatever I do is to help save your lives. God knows your souls are already in jeopardy.

SOLEDAD: Gimme a smoke, Lillie, will you? (LILLIAN *sneaks her one.*)

TESSIE: These drills scare me.

LILLIAN: Everything scares you. Come on, Einstein, you can hold my hand. (TESSIE *does.*)

SOLEDAD: God, I hate that sound.

RAMONITA: I hate this war.

ORQUIDEA: All right, ladies, heads up, backs straight! Down to the shelter we go! (*Marching to the head of the line.*) Hup, two, three, four . . . Hup, two, three, four . . . (*They begin to file out* SOLEDAD *in the rear.*) The last one out, get the lights. Hup, two, three, four . . . Hup, two, three, four . . . (*As* SOLEDAD *gets to the door, she marches in place a moment, then closes it, staying behind.* DOÑA ORQUIDEA *can still be heard outside counting out the march as* SOLEDAD *lights up the cigarette and inhales deeply, then exhales slowly as if relaxing for the first time. She takes out her make-up from her handbag and moves to the mirror, placing the photo of Marlene Dietrich next to her image. She begins trying to make herself resemble the actress, unaware of* ORQUIDEA *who has re-entered in a fury and stands watching her.* SOLEDAD *is taking great pains to get the lips just right, when suddenly* ORQUIDEA *blows her whistle loudly, causing her hand to jump and smear lipstick half across her face.*)

SOLEDAD: Jesus Christ, Mama! What did you do that for?

ORQUIDEA: Just testing your ears. Seeing whether or not you were deaf. Didn't you hear the siren before? But of course you heard the siren before. Everybody heard the siren before. Well if you heard the siren before, why didn't you follow me down to the shelter like you were supposed to?

SOLEDAD: I'm sorry, Mama. I was putting on my face.

ORQUIDEA: If that's the best you can do, I suggest you take it off again. (SOLEDAD *looks at her a moment then tries to repair her make-up.*) I don't understand what's wrong with you. I really don't. All you've ever cared about is how you looked. Even as a little girl all you ever cared about was how you looked.

SOLEDAD: That's not true, Mama.

ORQUIDEA: Don't tell me what's true and not true. I'll tell you what's true and not true. And what's true is that I am the Air Raid Warden and you don't care anything about it. About me! How can I expect for other people to follow my instructions when my own daughter refuses?

SOLEDAD: I said I was sorry. I made a mistake.

ORQUIDEA: Making mistakes is the story of your life! And put out that damned cigarette! I've told you how many times respectable women shouldn't smoke.

SOLEDAD: Yes, Mama. (*She puts out the cigarette.*)

161

ORQUIDEA: Just get downstairs before somebody notices. (*Like a drill sergeant.*) Move it, move it, move it!

SOLEDAD: (*Saluting.*) Yes, sir! (*She marches out.*) Hup, two, three, four. Hup, two, three, four . . .

ORQUIDEA: (*Watches her exit, then turns to the picture of Dietrich.*) You may fool my daughter, but you don't fool me. I don't care how many war bonds you've sold. (*She takes a marker from her table and draws a Hitler style moustache on the picture.*) Nazi bitch. (*She turns off the lights and exits. Blackout. In the darkness "Boogie Woogie Bugle Boy" by the Andrews Sisters begins.*)

ACT ONE

SCENE TWO

The music continues as the lights rise CS, which has been transformed to suggest SOLEDAD's living room. It is now Saturday morning and the music is coming from a phonograph placed atop a small cabinet over which a mirror hangs. SOLEDAD dressed in a skirt and halter top is cleaning up the apartment, periodically dancing to the music as she does. DOÑA ORQUIDEA enters from inside in her buttoned up nightclothes, carrying her rosary and her Bible.

SOLEDAD: Good morning, Mama.

ORQUIDEA: Have you learned all the words yet?

SOLEDAD: What, Mama?

ORQUIEDEA: To the song. Have you learned all the words yet? I know I have. After all, you've been playing it all morning. (*She turns off the phonograph.*) Do you want me to sing it for you?

SOLEDAD: Mama . . .

ORQUIDEA: (*Singing.*) He was a famous trumpet man from

down Chicago way;
He had a boogie style that no one else could play;
He was the top man at his craft . . .

SOLEDAD: You've made your point, Mama. I'm sorry. It's a new record. I thought you'd be up by now.

ORQUIDEA: Because I'm up doesn't mean I feel like jitter-bugging. You know I always pray in the morning. Though I doubt God could hear me today with all this racket. He was probably too busy dancing to listen.

SOLEDAD: Mama . . .

ORQUIDEA: And put some clothes on. Or are you planning to wear that brassiere to the Red Cross?

SOLEDAD: It's not a brassiere, Mama.

ORQUIDEA: For what it covers, it might as well be. Please, it's embarrassing enough for me having to look at your *tetas*, without having you show them off to the whole world as well. My God, I wouldn't be caught dead in such a thing.

SOLEDAD: I should hope not, Mama.

ORQUIDEA: Like you think you look so good? Well, what you look like is a *puta* . . . and a cheap one at that! You might as well be that Victoria or Lillian or that tramp of a mother of hers. Not one of you has any respect for anything proper. Anything decent . . . much less any respect for me!

SOLEDAD: What is it, Mama? Are you still angry about the air raid yesterday? Is that what this is really about?

ORQUIDEA: Why should I be angry because you made me look like a fool in front of everybody? You do it all the time.

SOLEDAD: Mama . . .

ORQUIDEA: These are bad times, Soledad. It is up to us to set the example. We are Puerto Ricans. We are ladies. That should mean something to you.

SOLEDAD: (*Moves to her sewing machine.*) I have to finish the dress I'm making for Evelyn. The only time I get to use the machine anymore is when you're not around.

ORQUIDEA: And why does the Princess need another dress?

Don't tell me she's actually changed her mind about coming home for my wedding?

SOLEDAD: She needs it for the big dance they have every year up at the camp, Mama. I told you. As it is, I hope it gets there in time.

ORQUIDEA: What happened to the one she wore last year?

SOLEDAD: She's grown up a lot, Mama. Most of her clothes are too babyish for her now. In case you haven't noticed, she's a young lady already.

ORQUIDEA: A spoiled brat is what she is.

SOLEDAD: Please, Mama, it's too early for this, okay? I didn't sleep too well last night. It's been a couple of weeks since I've heard from Armando and I'm starting to get worried. (*She looks up from her work.*) Are you sure you didn't write to him, Mama? Tell him something that would make him angry with me?

ORQUIDEA: All I've ever written him is the truth . . . And I told you to put on something decent. Don Felipe's bringing over some more of his things this morning and I don't want him seeing you in that. Or is it that you want him to think he's moving into a brothel?

SOLEDAD: I don't want him moving in here at all.

ORQUIDEA: And I don't want to hear any more about it! Armando said it would be okay and so that's that. That's the only permission I need . . . I really don't understand how you can be this way with Felipe. All he ever wanted was the best for you, Soledad. To be a good father to you.

SOLEDAD: Why don't you ever talk to me about my real father, Mama?

ORQUIDEA: Sometimes I think you're crazy, you know that? Why else would you want to bring him up now?

SOLEDAD: Because you never want to talk about him. You never have. Don't you think I have the right to know more about him than his rank? That he died?

ORQUIDEA: What more is there to know?

SOLEDAD: How he lived? What he was like? I don't even know if he wanted me. If he loved me.

ORQUIDEA: Of course he loved you.

SOLEDAD: Then tell me about him, Mama. Don't keep him all to yourself like you have. I want to love him too, but all he is now is an illusion. A ghost I spent my childhood making up stories about because I always felt like I never even had one.

ORQUIDEA: Oh, you had a father, all right. Lieutenant Robert F. Mallory. A great man. A great man who died in battle like so many lesser ones. (*She pauses a moment.*) Can't you understand it hurts me too much to talk about him? To unbury all of those memories? They're gone now. Ashes. Just like his body.

SOLEDAD: And so I'm left with nothing.

ORQUIDEA: Believe me, if, God forbid, Armando were to die there'd come a time you wouldn't want to talk about him either.

SOLEDAD: No matter how I felt about it myself, Mama, I'd want to make sure Evelyn knew all about him. That she'd remember him.

ORQUIDEA: Why? So the pain would never go away?

SOLEDAD: At least she'd feel something, which is more than I do a lot of the time.

ORQUIDEA: That's because you've never felt the loss of a husband . . . Tell me, what good would it do me to keep his memory alive? To light candles to it? To pay tribute by laying flowers on his grave? All it does is make you see how little you have in the present. What a deception your own mortality is. Why can't you just forget about the Lieutenant and accept Felipe as your father?

SOLEDAD: Because he's not! (*She watches* ORQUIDEA *a moment, sensing her pain, then slowly moves to her.*) I'm sorry, Mama . . . (*She gently touches her; however,* OR-QUIDEA *stiffens and quickly moves away.*)

ORQUIDEA: I'd better get dressed myself. I don't want Don Felipe to see me in this either. He might get ideas. And put something on already! I will not walk down the street with you all exposed like that, much less walk into Red Cross.

SOLEDAD: I told you yesterday I wasn't going with you today, Mama.

ORQUIDEA: (*Panicked.*) And what am I supposed to do? You know I hate taking the subway alone. What if I get lost?

SOLEDAD: You've been here twenty years, Mama. You won't get lost. If you want I'll pin your name and address on you like I used to do for Evelyn. Or ask Don Felipe to take you. God knows he does little else.

ORQUIDEA: And what do you plan to do instead? Waste your time going to the movies with Victoria again?

SOLEDAD: No, Mama, as a matter of fact I'm having company. I invited the girls over this afternoon.

ORQUIDEA: What? So this is what you meant by wanting to be alone? I should have known you were up to something. You always did place your friends above the truth. Above everything. I just hope you didn't take it into your head to invite that Victoria.

SOLEDAD: No, Mama, I wouldn't subject her to maybe running into you.

ORQUIDEA: No, of course not. She's so wonderful. But I'm sure that Lillian will be here.

SOLEDAD: Why woudn't I invite her, Mama? She lives three blocks away.

ORQUIDEA: Well, show me who you walk with and I'll know with whom you sleep.

SOLEDAD: There's nothing wrong with my friends, Mama. They're a bunch of nice women, that's all.

ORQUIDEA: Nice women don't spend all of their time talking about men.

SOLEDAD: When they haven't seen their husbands in two years, they sure do.

ORQUIDEA: Well not in my time. And not in Puerto Rico.

SOLEDAD: I know. In Puerto Rico you and your friends sat around and prayed all day. Well, this isn't Puerto Rico, Mama. And in case you've forgotten, my friends are the only ones who helped me when we came here. Who didn't try to beat me up every time I stepped foot out of the door.

ORQUIDEA: It's always difficult for anybody in a new country, but it is up to that person to show the others who they really are. To let them see their breeding. But not you. No. You preferred to let everybody think you were nothing more than white trash.

SOLEDAD: You're the only one who thought that, Mama. Everybody else thought I was a lousy spic.

ORQUIDEA: Had you not associated yourself with negroes and tramps, they wouldn't have.

SOLEDAD: You seem to find my friends good enough for the factory. To even ask some of them to be in your wedding party.

ORQUIDEA: To please you! And look at how you repaid me. By refusing to even participate in it!

SOLEDAD: Really? I thought it was because your own friends turned you down. That the ladies at the church all thought it was a little ridiculous.

ORQUIDEA: That's not true! (*After a pause.*) What is ridiculous is your even thinking of having a party what with Armando overseas. What with him maybe giving up his life at this very moment like your father did. Fighting for what's right in this world! For what's decent in this life!

SOLEDAD: It's not my fault he went, Mama. I didn't ask him to re-enlist.

ORQUIDEA: It was his duty to go. His obligation as a man!

SOLEDAD: And what about his obligation to me? He had already been in the service, Mama. The least he could have done was wait to see if he'd be called up again. But no, the minute his friends joined, he was right there saluting along with them!

ORQUIDEA: What was he supposed to do? Stay home like a coward?

SOLEDAD: Stay home and look after his family! Stay home and stay alive! Sometimes I feel like just running away. Like taking Evelyn and not being here when he gets back. Show him what it feels like to be left alone.

ORQUIDEA: You act like you're the only woman whose husband ever went off to war. Well, if you were really worried about Armando you wouldn't be wasting your time making parties for your friends. Making dresses for your daughter. Wasting his allotment checks buying stupid records for yourself!

SOLEDAD: I bought two lousy records, Mama. Don't make it sound like I bought out R.C.A. Victor! (ORQUIDEA *can only glare at her.*) Instead of always criticizing everybody, why don't you ever take a look at yourself? You're out there helping any stranger in uniform, yet your own granddaughter, your own flesh and blood, you begrudge a lousy home-made dress. Don't you ever think that maybe she might like something from you?

ORQUIDEA: You had her, you raise her!

SOLEDAD: Fine! But the next time you're buying yourself those fancy little chocolates you and Don Felipe love so much, think a little about the daughter you had and try paying part of the rent here for a change.

ORQUIDEA: You've had a job and you've got an allotment check! That more than covers the rent! But you don't want to hear that, do you? No! All you want to hear is your boogie woogies!

SOLEDAD: Can't you understand that I am tired of listening to either *danzas* that went out twenty years ago or romantic *boleros* that only depress me now?

ORQUIDEA: Since when have you ever found love songs depressing?

SOLEDAD: Since Armando re-enlisted and you moved back in

on me! Any more questions?

ORQUIDEA: You know perfectly well that wasn't my idea! Armando made me promise . . . No . . . Armando begged me to promise to stay here and keep an eye on you.

SOLEDAD: And did he beg Don Felipe, too?

ORQUIDEA: What's the matter? Are you jealous of my happiness or that Armando trusts me? That he wants me around?

SOLEDAD: I just want to know why nobody's ever bothered asking me what I wanted.

ORQUIDEA: Because he is the head of the house! He is the man! He makes all the decisions!

SOLEDAD: (*To end the argument.*) Fine, Mama, whatever you say! Whatever you say!

ORQUIDEA: Listen, since I'm such an aggravation to you I can leave right now. I'll go inside and write to him . . . I'll tell him that I'm very sorry . . . That I tried . . . That I did my best . . . But that for some reason you don't want me here . . . Strange as though it might seem for a daughter to act that way with her mother, especially a week before her wedding! Especially when she's already doing everything she can to destroy it! And not because it's to Don Felipe, but out of spite. To try and degrade me on what should be the happiest day of my life!

SOLEDAD: Will you stop it already! Haven't I got enough to worry about with Armando without having to listen to you go on and on about your damned wedding twenty-four hours a day? (ORQUIDEA's *only response is to stare back at her.*) Please, Mama, enough. Okay? I'm tired of fighting with you.

ORQUIDEA: So am I. Especially about things you have no right to criticize. (*She exits inside.*)

SOLEDAD: I swear, Armando, if you come out of this war alive, I'm going to kill you! (*Blackout. In the darkness the introduction to "Bésame Mucho" can be heard.*)

ACT ONE

SCENE THREE

The music continues full blast as the lights rise on RAMONITA's *kitchen, DSR, where* CARLOTTA *is washing the wall, screeching her rendition of the song playing on the radio. It is still Saturday morning and* RAMONITA *is seated at the small table cluttered with candles, dishes, herbs, a glass of water turned upside down on a saucer, etc., drinking a cup of coffee as she reads over some carefully kept old letters. An assortment of* CARLOTTA's *clothing is slung over the back of her chair, as well as is her large handbag.*

CARLOTTA: (*Screeching.*) ¡Bésame! ¡Bésame el culo!

RAMONITA: Carlotta!

CARLOTTA: (*In her own world.*) ¡Como si fuera esta noche la última vez!

RAMONITA: Carlotta!

CARLOTTA: ¡Bésame! ¡Bésame el culo!

RAMONITA: Carlotta, please!

CARLOTTA: What?

RAMONITA: Shut up and lower that! We're gonna get evicted!

CARLOTTA: It's not that loud!

RAMONITA: No? They can hear you back in Havana!

CARLOTTA: Okay! Okay! Don't have a conniption! (*She turns off the radio.*) Had I known the Bronx was so quiet I never would have moved up here.

RAMONITA: It's not that the Bronx is quiet, it's that you're very loud. The other night when I was coming home I could hear you carrying on from three blocks away.

CARLOTTA: I like to sing. What's wrong with that?

RAMONITA: You sound like somebody's strangling you, that's what. Last week old Mrs. Zimmerman on the ground floor almost called the police. She swore you were being murdered. And she's deaf! She doesn't even hear fire engines!

CARLOTTA: Ahh, you just don't know talent. I always thought I should be a singer. Carlotta Lacube! It sounds too exotic to just work in a factory. (*She takes a sip from her coffee and begins to gag and cough.*) *Ave María*, are you trying to kill me?

RAMONITA: What's the matter with you now?

CARLOTTA: It's not me, honey. What's the matter with this coffee?

RAMONITA: What can I tell you? It's that time of the month.

CARLOTTA: What? The coffee pot's having its period?

RAMONITA: No, you idiot. We're just out of sugar is all. I had to use Karo syrup.

CARLOTTA: Why didn't you say something? (*She takes out two restaurant sugarbowls from her bag and sings, using them like maracas.*) "Oh Tico Tico Tick, Oh Tico Tico Tick." Compliments of Horn and Hardart. No wonder my bag was so heavy. I've been carrying them around for a week.

RAMONITA: One of these days you're going to be arrested.

CARLOTTA: (*As she's about to take a sip of coffee.*) I can't wait for this lousy war to be over so I can finally have a cup of coffee that's not green.

RAMONITA: I don't mind it so much.

CARLOTTA: You don't seem to mind nothing lately. Not even those horrible dresses Orquídea wants us to wear. Why I said I'd be a bridesmaid is beyond me. I think I was just so shocked that she asked me. Can you imagine what I'm gonna look like in that rag?

RAMONITA: Don't worry so much about it. You're gonna look beautiful.

CARLOTTA: In orange satin I'm either gonna look like a pumpkin or a prostitute. My God, I've seen voodoo dolls dressed more tastefully.

RAMONITA: Just be glad we convinced her out of the red, white, and blue ones.

CARLOTTA: Only she could think of a patriotic wedding. (*She takes another sip of coffee.*) Forget it. I'd rather drink the ammonia. At least that doesn't need sugar. (*She notices the glass of water.*) *Carajo*, just look at all these bubbles. (*Raising her arms as she screams.*) *Coño*! Whoever's thinking evil about me should . . . ! (*Catches herself and becomes calm.*) No. Whatever evil thoughts are meant for me should go back to the sender. And to their mother! (*She looks at* RAMONITA *a moment.*) Why don't you put those away? They're just gonna get you more depressed.

RAMONITA: I'd amost forgotten how poetic Ralfie could be sometimes.

CARLOTTA: Honey, I know you don't believe in things like I do, but somehow I know inside Ralfie's going to be okay. I can feel it.

RAMONITA: Yeah. He's going to be fine.

CARLOTTA: (*Starts back to her washing.*) I'd better hurry up with this if we're ever gonna get out of here.

RAMONITA: We don't have to be at Soledad's until one.

CARLOTTA: I know, but I have to stop off at a Hunsixteenth Street on the way. I promised cousin Olga I'd do another session for her tomorrow and I have to pick up something from the *botánica* there. Besides, I saw the cutest little hat in the store right next to it. I've been praying all week it's still there.

RAMONITA: You and your hats.

CARLOTTA: I don't know why Olga has me come over though. I tell her the same thing week after week. "Nothing has happened to you. Nothing is happening to you. And nothing is ever going to happen to you." *Bendito*, she's so boring even the spirits don't want to have anything to do with her. I was thinking of telling her I had a vision she should move back to Cuba.

RAMONITA: I'd pay for her ticket. I just can't believe how angry people get over things they don't even understand!

Being a pacifist doesn't make you unamerican. If we cared anything about this world we never would have let things get this far. We'd have tried to stop the killing before it ever began. Wars aren't fought about people, Carlotta. There'd be some honor in that. Wars are big business, as much for our side as for theirs. Why do you think we wanted it so badly?

CARLOTTA: Nobody wants war.

RAMONITA: No, everybody wants peace. However there's no profit in that. Believe me, Carlotta, death is as much of a product as those damned blouses we sew, only now it's government issued. And it's about time you, me, and the rest of the world stopped buying it.

CARLOTTA: Maybe you're right. I don't know. Like I don't know how two grown up women can get one apartment so dirty.

RAMONITA: It would help if you were a little less sloppy.

CARLOTTA: Me? Name me one thing I do that's sloppy?

RAMONITA: All right. First, you never make your bed. Second, you leave your clothes lying all around for me to pick up after you. Third, you leave your dirty dishes wherever you happen to be eating, including the bathroom. Fourth, you leave your candles burning here, and your glasses of water there, and your powders and your potions . . .

CARLOTTA: Listen, I said one thing. I didn't ask you to read me the telephone book.

RAMONITA: You wanted to know.

CARLOTTA: Okay, so now I know. I'm not only loud, I'm a pig.

RAMONITA: That's not what I said.

CARLOTTA: (*A bit tentatively.*) Speaking of leaving things lying around, whose clothes were those in the living room last night?

RAMONITA: What clothes?

CARLOTTA: The khaki number. Usually comes with a soldier attached.

RAMONITA: I don't know what you're talking about.

CARLOTTA: I may have been a little tipsy when I came in, but I wasn't exactly seeing pink elephants either. What I saw was a man's uniform lying by the couch with nobody in it.

RAMONITA: So what if you did? I just had a friend come over for a while.

CARLOTTA: Your friends don't usually get naked on the sofa.

RAMONITA: Will you stop with the third degree? You'd swear you were my husband or something.

CARLOTTA: I don't have to be your husband to worry about you.

RAMONITA: Well, don't!

CARLOTTA: Ramonita . . . I only mentioned it because I was surprised. I've been living with you for over a year now. Ever since Ralfie disappeared . . . And you have to admit it's not like you to do something like that.

RAMONITA: Why not? I don't have a right to be lonely? Or don't you know what loneliness is?

CARLOTTA: *¡Mira, yo no sé lo que te está pasando, pero para ya!* You know damned well I know what it's like to be lonely. Probably a hell of a lot better than you do! Or do you think it's easy for a woman like me? At least you have somebody, whether he's here with you or not.

RAMONITA: (*After a pause.*) I'm sorry.

CARLOTTA: (*Another pause.*) So, who is he? I doubt you met him at your women's club.

RAMONITA: I don't know.

CARLOTTA: What do you mean you don't know?

RAMONITA: Just what I said. I didn't want to know his name. I didn't want to know anything about him.

CARLOTTA: Then why go to bed with him?

RAMONITA: (*Pause.*) He looked so much like Ralfie.

CARLOTTA: Oh, honey . . .

RAMONITA: I met him yesterday when I was at the V.A. Shit!

There I am looking for my husband and what do I do? Make a date with a total stranger just because he looks like him!

CARLOTTA: (*A slight pause.*) Maybe if you believed a little more . . .

RAMONITA: In what? Voices of the dead? Or in a God that lets people slaughter each other? That lets an entire world go crazy for bloodshed? That lets my husband vanish like he was never even alive!

CARLOTTA: You've got to believe that he'll come home to you.

RAMONITA: And if he does, then what? We just pretend the war has never happened?

CARLOTTA: (*After a pause she takes a sip of coffee.*) You know, this coffee's not so bad when it gets cold. (*They sit there silently a moment. Blackout. In the darkness the song "Cachita" begins.*)

ACT ONE

SCENE FOUR

The music continues as the lights rise DSL, on LILLIAN *and* TESSIE *in their apartment, late Saturday morning.* LILLIAN *is trying to teach her the rhumba; however, despite her urgings,* TESSIE *seems more to be dancing with her shoulders than anything else.*

LILLIAN: Come on, Tessie, it's the rhumba, not the samba! Leave your shoulders alone! Shake the bottom, not the top!

TESSIE: I'll never get it.

LILLIAN: Just follow me. Step together and step together and step . . . (TESSIE *continues with her shoulders.*) Hey, Carmen Miranda, if you've got to shake something, use what you've got. (*She begins shaking her shoulders, causing her breasts to bounce.*) Like that, honey. Bounce them all over the dancefloor!

TESSIE: Forget it. There's nothing here to bounce. Anyway, I've got to finish painting my legs.

LILLIAN: Don't you think you should shave them first?

TESSIE: I did!

LILLIAN: Then try using a razor next time, not a butterknife.

TESSIE: Oh, gin crackers! (*She begins applying the pancake make-up to her legs; however, as she lifts her skirt we see she has already painted on a garter belt.*)

LILLIAN: (*Picking up her drink.*) It'll be like old times getting together with Soledad. She hasn't really entertained since her mother moved back in. But you should have seen the fun times we used to have. Her, me, and Ramonita. Back in school we were inseparable.

TESSIE: I know all about "The Terrible Trio." Still, I thought you didn't like Ramonita?

LILLIAN: I'm talking about before she married that creep Ralfie and became everybody's conscience.

TESSIE: You have to expect people to change once they get married, even I know that. Most husbands are jealous of their wives' old girlfriends. I know Skippy sure was.

LILLIAN: I don't know why, Tessie, but every time you mention Skippy, for some reason I keep picturing a cocker spaniel.

TESSIE: I've told you not to say that! Skippy was not a dog! His real name was Edmundo. Skippy was just my pet name for him.

LILLIAN: (*Takes a sip from her drink.*) I'm just glad the old battle-ax won't be there today. If I hear one more thing about her lousy wedding I'm gonna puke. I swear, a woman Orquídea's age going around like a blushing bride is not only absurd, it's demented.

TESSIE: You're just angry because you're not in the bridal party.

LILLIAN: Sweetheart, I didn't want to be in my own bridal party, much less the Orchid's.

TESSIE: Well, I feel bad for her. Soledad really should be her matron of honor, not that I don't consider it an honor myself to be asked.

LILLIAN: You honestly like the witch.

TESSIE: She's not a witch, even though she does scare the begeezes out of me sometimes when she starts talking about hell and the devil. She makes it sound so real.

LILLIAN: I just can't figure out why she's remarrying the bum. I hope to God it's not for sex. Can you imagine that picture?

TESSIE: Oh, I don't think they have sex. They're too religious. I'm sure it's just their way of making up to God for breaking their wedding vows.

LILLIAN: Well, vows or no vows, you would think with all her pride she'd be too embarrassed to go back to a man that divorced her. Especially to go off and live with another woman. I know if Manolo did that to me, I'd never want to see the creep's face again, much less remarry him.

TESSIE: Not even if he realized his mistake? If he came crawling back to you like Don Felipe did? I don't know, I'd find it romantic.

LILLIAN: To hear you talk you'd think Don Felipe was Don Ameche.

TESSIE: Not all men are creeps, you know. Skippy wasn't. And take Armando.

LILLIAN: I would if I could. (*She freshens her drink.*)

TESSIE: Didn't you have enough of those last night?

LILLIAN: Yeah, but this is today.

TESSIE: I thought you were on a diet.

LILLIAN: I am. Didn't you see me eat that grapefruit this morning?

TESSIE: After swallowing a mountain of flapjacks.

LILLIAN: Well, every little bit helps. Rome wasn't built in a day, you know.

TESSIE: Obviously neither was your body. And then with all the alcohol you put in it . . .

LILLIAN: What can I tell you? This is how they like me . . .

Fat and sassy.

TESSIE: Nobody likes fat people.

LILLIAN: Nobody likes dumb broads either. Especially when they've got no teeth.

TESSIE: Don't blow a gasket. I'm just telling you for your own good. Maybe if you did lose some weight, Manolo would even treat you better.

LILLIAN: I lost weight for Manolo once. The louse didn't even notice. And when he finally did, he thought it was because I was cheating on him.

TESSIE: Then do it for yourself.

LILLIAN: I do all right for myself as it is. In fact, had you not left the dance so early last night, you'd know those two jarheads we were talking to came back over and bought the rest of my drinks.

TESSIE: Which two? We yakked to a lot more than two marines. Oh, wait a minute. Not the hunk who looked like Gary Cooper?

LILLIAN: Bullseye!

TESSIE: And the Latin doll with the eyebrows like Victor Mature?

LILLIAN: I tell you, I haven't heard men whisper things like that to me in ages. I was ready to take them both on at once.

TESSIE: Sometimes you act like a real tramp, you know that?

LILLIAN: Me? What was all that with you and Joe again? You two were stuck together like fly paper.

TESSIE: He's shipping out soon. He just needed somebody to talk to.

LILLIAN: He's been using that line on you for the last three months! And last night you were doing a lot more than talking, sweetheart.

TESSIE: Oh, peppers!

LILLIAN: Yeah? Well, lately you seem to get his peppers red hot! . . . not to mention his sausage. The bouncer was about to throw a pail of hot water on you to see if you two came apart.

TESSIE: That's a lot of hooey.

LILLIAN: I really wish you wouldn't use words like that. It makes me feel like I'm living with Ginger Rogers.

TESSIE: Put a sock in it, Lillie. (*Trying to change the subject, she hands* LILLIAN *an eyebrow pencil.*) Here, draw the lines for me. And make sure the seams look straight this time. (*She stands on a chair.*)

LILLIAN: (*As she draws the seams down the back of* TESSIE's *legs.*) Why don't you get a decent pair of silk ones already?

TESSIE: Mrs. Master Sergeant Edmundo Minero shopping on the black market? Never. It says in the paper every day that it's just like giving money to the enemy.

LILLIAN: Fine. Then go around looking like you've got wooden legs.

TESSIE: Anyway, they cost too much.

LILLIAN: I swear, Tessie, you are so cheap.

TESSIE: I am not cheap! I'm on a budget. And stockings are just not part of it.

LILLIAN: Well, then talk to Joe. I'm sure you two could work something out.

TESSIE: You're not actually suggesting I trade my body for a pair of stockings?

LILLIAN: Not trade it, Tessie, lend it out to him for an hour or two. Who's to know?

TESSIE: I suppose next you'll ask me to go for a Hershey bar!

LILLIAN: No. And not just for one lousy pair of lousy stockings, either. Make sure he at least throws in a couple of pounds of sugar or something.

TESSIE: I can't believe my ears.

LILLIAN: Grow up already.

TESSIE: I'm very sorry, Lillian, but the wife of Master Sergeant Minero could never do anything like that.

LILLIAN: (*Not paying attention to her work, she draws the seams crooked.*) Then poor Skippy must have died horny as hell. After all, what do you think he was fighting for?

TESSIE: His country, like everybody else.

LILLIAN: No, sweetie, he was fighting for your country . . . without the r and the y.

TESSIE: (*Thinks about this a minute, then it hits her.*) Oh my God, that's filthy!

LILLIAN: Then I suggest you wash it. Or don't they do that in Buenos Aires?

TESSIE: (*Blessing herself.*) Hail Mary, Mother of God, pray for this sinner now and at the hour of her death, which may be any minute now . . .

LILLIAN: (*Dragging her out by the arm.*) Come on. Let's go.

TESSIE: (*Turning back for a moment, to finish her prayer.*) Amen! (*Blackout. In the darkness the danza "Luz María" by Raphael Hernández begins.*)

ACT ONE

SCENE FIVE

The music continues as the lights rise on SOLEDAD's *apartment that afternoon, where she and* LILLIAN *watch from the sidelines as* ORQUIDEA *pins up the hem on the green ruffled gown* TESSIE *is wearing. A few cartons are now stacked in the corner.* CARLOTTA *and* RAMONITA *are also there in their very ruffled orange bridesmaids gowns; however,* ORQUIDEA *and* TESSIE *seem to be the only ones enjoying themselves. The others are sitting around drinking their Coca Colas, bored out of their minds with the music and with* ORQUIDEA, *especially* CARLOTTA *who is having trouble staying awake, her new little red hat perched precariously on her head.*

TESSIE: That's a swell record, Doña Orquídea.

ORQUIDEA: I brought it with me from Puerto Rico.

CARLOTTA: (*Suppressing a yawn.*) Aren't we lucky?

LILLIAN: (*To* SOLEDAD.) I thought Florence Nightingale was going to the Red Cross.

SOLEDAD: And leave me to have a good time? Can you believe, she's scared to go out alone? As if anybody would actually start with her.

TESSIE: I'm so glad you're here today, Doña Orquídea. I was sure hoping you'd be.

ORQUIDEA: I figured as long as you ladies were coming over, I'd better use the time to make sure all of your dresses fit properly.

CARLOTTA: Can I take this off already? I'm afraid I might wrinkle it.

ORQUIDEA: Get up and move around a bit. Get used to how it feels. This way you'll be more comfortable.

SOLEDAD: Something tells me she'd be more comfortable home in bed in her pajamas.

LILLIAN: Really, Carlotta, that dress is you! Orange is definitely your color. Why, I've never seen you look so . . . alive!

CARLOTTA: I know. And it's so practical, too. Just think of all the places I can wear it later.

TESSIE: Yeah. I bet we'd make a big hit at the Palladium in these.

LILLIAN: In those you'd make a big hit anywhere. I can't wait to see your gown, Doña Orquídea. What color is it? Chartreuse?

TESSIE: This is so exciting! I feel almost like it's me who's getting married. I tell you, this is gonna be some wedding, Doña Orquídea. I bet you're gonna make some bride.

ORQUIDEA: I wish you would have seen my first wedding, Tessie. I was so young then. Just a girl . . . barely sixteen years old . . . In a dress my mother made for me by hand. All silk and lace with beads the color of ivory. Nobody had ever seen a dress like that before. Even the priest told me I was the most beautiful bride that had ever graced his church. That it was his honor to marry me. And my father . . . why he was so proud of me, he invited not only my family and friends, but all of Río Piedras to come and celebrate my happiness. We had money back then. People respected themselves and each other. Now nobody respects anything anymore. It's as dead as my lieutenant the day they returned him to me in that pine box covered by a flag.

TESSIE: I bet he was some man, Doña Orquídea. A hero, just like Skippy.

ORQUIDEA: Yes, a hero.

TESSIE: Golly, I could listen to you talk for hours.

LILLIAN: We just have.

ORQUIDEA: (*Placing the final pin in* TESSIE*'s gown.*) There, that should do it.

TESSIE: Look at me everybody! Don't I look like a Princess?

LILLIAN: You look more like a pea. (ORQUIDEA *shoots her a look.*)

TESSIE: Put on that record again, Doña Orquidea, so I can see how it moves when I dance.

ORQUIDEA: All right, Tessie. (*She starts towards the phonograph.*)

SOLEDAD: Please, Mama, not again. You're putting everybody to sleep.

CARLOTTA: (*Awaking with a start.*) No, don't worry about me. I'm having a wonderful time.

ORQUIDEA: Oh, I forgot. Only you can play a record more than once. Well, fine! Go ahead. Put on whatever you want. You're going to anyway.

CARLOTTA: Thank God.

TESSIE: Have you got any Vaughn Monroe? Skippy just loved Vaughn Monroe. (SOLEDAD *ignores her and puts on "In the Mood" by Glenn Miller.*)

LILLIAN: Oh, Glenn, baby . . .

SOLEDAD: Come on, Lillie, dance with me. I'll lead.

CARLOTTA: *Dios mío*, I feel like a piñata.

LILLIAN: It must feel good being free of the kid for a while.

SOLEDAD: To tell you the truth, I miss her like crazy. Still I'm glad she's not around for this circus. It's just a shame they don't have a camp I can send my mother to. Now I know what it's like to be a prisoner of war.

LILLIAN: You think so? Well imagine when Don Felipe moves in? I don't even know why you're letting that happen.

SOLEDAD: I guess I just keep hoping it won't. That one of them will get hit by a bus or something.

LILLIAN: Hoping ain't gonna change anything. If it did, right now I'd be a size five and you'd be Cary Grant. (*As if to stop from thinking,* SOLEDAD *really gets into the music and begins doing somewhat of a solo.*) That's right. Show me up.

TESSIE: Boy, I sure wish I could dance like that.

ORQUIDEA: You call that dancing? (LILLIAN *gets back into the dance and the two continue having their good time, much to* ORQUIDEA*'s displeasure.*) You would think at her weight she would want to hide her body instead of bouncing it around like that. I really don't know how you can tolerate living with her.

TESSIE: Well, these past two years haven't been easy. And now since the wedding . . . I think she's really hurt you didn't ask her to be a bridesmaid. She hasn't said anything, but I'm sure she is.

ORQUIDEA: Please, it's bad enough Carlotta walked in when I was asking you and Ramonita. The woman looked so excited I didn't have the heart to tell her no. She just assumed I meant her, too.

TESSIE: So did Lillie. She was with her.

ORQUIDEA: That's different. Be sensible, Tessie. You know yourself, Lillie, doesn't know how to behave, not that Carlotta's much better. Still, at least some people might find her attractive. But Lillian? She's just like her mother, that one. The two of them, man-crazy, sex maniacs.

TESSIE: You're so funny, Doña Orquídea. Her mother's been

in a wheelchair for the last twenty years. How can she possibly be a sex-maniac?

ORQUIDEA: You never know with people of her class. And she wasn't always crippled. Though she might as well have been for all the good she's done. Just look at the daughter she raised. It's inconceivable I ever let Soledad talk me into giving her a job. I don't care how good she sews. (*She begins unpacking a carton of white plaster religious statues.*)

TESSIE: It really means a lot to her. Manolo sends his allotment check to his mother. Without this job she'd have nothing.

ORQUIDEA: (*Watches them dance a moment longer.*) Will you two sit down already! You look like two lesbians!

SOLEDAD: Oh, Mama.

ORQUIDEA: I can't help it if it looks funny for women to dance together.

LILLIAN: What about the Rockettes?

TESSIE: Don't say anything bad about the Rockettes. I love them even more than Fred and Ginger.

CARLOTTA: I had an aunt who did that. Danced a lot with other women. Nobody was too surprised when she finally left her husband for one.

ORQUIDEA: *¡Qué asco!*

TESSIE: (*To* LILLIAN.) I'd rather die than go to bed with a woman. What could you even do?

LILLIAN: What are you asking me for? I look like a lezzie?

SOLEDAD: (*Noticing* ORQUIDEA.) Must you do that now, Mama?

ORQUIDEA: I'm just showing them to Tessie. We're thinking of using them as the centerpieces at the reception.

LILLIAN: Well, it's original. Still, they look a little pale to me.

ORQUIDEA: (*Frustrated.*) Don Felipe hasn't painted them yet.

LILLIAN: Oh, yeah. I forgot that's what he does. Do you think he'd let me pose for one? I'd love to have a virgin with my face on it.

ORQUIDEA: He paints saints, Lillian. He doesn't perform miracles.

LILLIAN: Oh, that was a good one. But just between us, don't you think you're doing up this wedding just a teensy bit much? I mean, most people third time down the aisle would settle for a nice simple civil affair. I'd have thought you'd put all this money into war bonds or something.

ORQUIDEA: What I do with my money is no concern of yours. And I am doing it for the war. The war on the homefront. The war for morality . . . or what's left of it. Which reminds me, ladies, Monday ends the clothesdrive and still not one of you has given me any of your old clothes yet.

LILLIAN: Believe me, Doña Orquídea, any old clothes I've got, I'm wearing.

ORQUIDEA: And what about the poor Italians? What are they supposed to do?

LILLIAN: Screw 'em. Let them wear spaghetti for all I give a damn.

ORQUIDEA: I will not allow you to talk that way in my presence! CARLOTTA: (*Indicating her bridesmaid dress.*) They can have this next week.

ORQUIDEA: I don't understand you women. You would think we were still fighting against them.

LILLIAN: We're not? Then what was Manolo doing at Anzio?

ORQUIDEA: But we've beaten them already. Our war with them is over.

LILLIAN: Since when all of a sudden do you like the Italians so much?

ORQUIDEA: It's Archbishop Spellman who's collecting the clothes, not me. After all, they are Catholics.

RAMONITA: Somebody should tell your Archbishop Spellman there . . .

LILLIAN: Oh God, she woke up.

RAMONITA: Somebody should tell your Archbishop Spellman that instead of collecting clothes for the Italians, he should be telling the Pope to finally do something about what's happening to the Jews over there.

TESSIE: Don't say anything bad about the Pope . . .

RAMONITA: I know, you love him even more than Fred and Ginger too, right?

LILLIAN: If you ask me, you should be more worried about your husband than about any Jews. Let them take care of their own.

RAMONITA: Because I'm worried about Ralfie doesn't mean I have to stop caring about the rest of the world. They are your neighbors, you know.

LILLIAN: Some neighbors. The minute Manolo and I moved in they started flying out. They don't like the Spanish any better than I like them.

RAMONITA: Did you ever think that maybe it wasn't because you were Spanish? That maybe it was because . . .

LILLIAN: Don't say it. Don't even think it, sister, or you're gonna be picking up your teeth all over Eighth Avenue!

SOLEDAD: Hey, you two, come on. We're supposed to be having a good time, remember?

RAMONITA: Some things are more important than just having a good time.

SOLEDAD: I know that, Ramonita, but please, not today. Today I don't want to think about my problems. Believe me, I'll have plenty of time tomorrow to think about them.

RAMONITA: Fine, Miss Scarlett. Why don't you just move back to Tara?

SOLEDAD: Ramonita, please. It's my anniversary today, all right?

RAMONITA: Your anniversary?

CARLOTTA: But why didn't you say something? We would have had you a party.

SOLEDAD: I thought that's what we were having.

LILLIAN: I'm sorry, Soledad. I forgot, too.

SOLEDAD: Don't worry, so did my mother.

ORQUIDEA: Are you kidding? It's you who I thought forgot.

SOLEDAD: How could I ever forget my wedding, Mama? (*After a pause.*) Hey, come on, let's pick this party up! Who needs something?

LILLIAN: Me, a drink. Preferably one with a little kick to it.

CARLOTTA: In this house? Are you crazy?

SOLEDAD: Oh, yeah? (*She takes a bottle of rum from inside the cabinet.*) Well, ladies, feast your eyes on this!

CARLOTTA: Thank you, Santa Barbara!

ORQUIDEA: Where did you get that from? Don't tell me you actually went into a liquor store yourself?

LILLIAN: Who cares where she got it? Just so long as it's here. (*She holds out her glass.*) Anchors aweigh, kiddo!

SOLEDAD: (*As she pours LILLIE's drink.*) Anybody else? (*The women each hold out their glasses respectively.*)

TESSIE: I really shouldn't.

CARLOTTA: Me neither.

RAMONITA: What the hell. (SOLEDAD *pours the rum into their glasses.*)

SOLEDAD: Mama? (ORQUIDEA *just stares at her, seething.*) Well, ladies, what shall we drink to?

RAMONITA: To your anniversary, of course.

TESSIE: And to your mother's wedding.

SOLEDAD: No, Tessie, let's find something we can all enjoy.

CARLOTTA: (*Toasting.*) To Clark Gable. May he come walking through that door right now, stark naked!

LILLIAN: I'll drink to that.

TESSIE: You'll drink to anything.

SOLEDAD: I've got it. (*Toasting.*) To us! Women without men! May our boys all come home soon!

CARLOTTA: Amen. (*The women drink up.*)

LILLIAN: Now that's what a Coke should taste like! Hit me again, Soledad. Only leave out the cola this time. (*Blackout. In the darkness we hear the opening chords of "Don't Sit Under The Apple Tree" by the Andrews Sisters. The lights rise on the women, drunk on their faces, as they sing, laugh and dance, passing the half empty bottly between them, much to* ORQUIDEA's *chagrin.*)

ACT ONE

SCENE SIX

As the women half collapse in laughter,

TESSIE: (*Over the others.*) I don't think I'm going to make it to see Joe Joe tonight!

LILLIAN: I don't think you're gonna make it out the front door tonight!

TESSIE: Who cares? I feel so good!

LILLIAN: Wait till you see how you feel tomorrow.

TESSIE: Come on, Orquídea, get up and dance!

ORQUIDEA: No.

SOLEDAD: Oh, come on, Mama. If you're gonna be here, at least join the fun! (*She takes her by the arm; however,* ORQUIDEA *roughly pulls away.*) ORQUIDEA: Will you let go of me? Don't touch me! Just leave me alone!

LILLIAN: You know, Doña Orquídea, maybe if you did have a drink you might loosen up a little.

ORQUIDEA: I'm sorry if it offends you, ladies; I can't jump around like an idiot while your husbands may be lying dead in a foxhole somewhere.

LILLIAN: Believe me, Doña Orquídea, if Manolo's lying in any foxhole, the only thing he's doing is trying to hump it. That or whacking any Wac who's stupid enough to be there with him.

ORQUIDEA: If you have no respect for yourself or your husband, I demand you at least have some respect for me!

SOLEDAD: To tell you the truth, Mama, I don't know how much I respect any of them right now either. Armando included. Somehow I can't help but feel that if they really didn't enjoy it, they wouldn't have all been so willing to get up and join the fight. I can't help but feel it's like playing cops and robbers to them, only now they get to use real bullets.

ORQUIDEA: When we win you'll see how differently you'll feel. You'll see that it's us who have God on our side. When we win you'll be as proud of all of them as I am!

SOLEDAD: I've already lost two years of my marriage. My child, two years of her father. Tell me, Mama, when we win what prize do we get that makes up for all we've already lost?

LILLIAN: I need a refill.

SOLEDAD: Me, too.

ORQUIDEA: Haven't you had enough?

SOLEDAD: Drinks? No.

TESSIE: I've got a better idea. Why don't we all go to the beach tomorrow? I know I could sure use a tan.

ORQUIDEA: Don't you know too much sun is bad for you?

TESSIE: But I'm so white!

ORQUIDEA: You should be happy you're white.

CARLOTTA: There's nothing wrong with a little color, Doña Orquídea. After all, look at me.

ORQUIDEA: That's different. Everybody expects for Cubans to be black.

CARLOTTA: Listen, I'm not exactly Aunt Jemima, you know? I am caramel. Sweet and delicious.

LILLIAN: Just don't stand near any organ grinders. In that hat somebody may put a nickel in your hand.

CARLOTTA: Oh, shut up, you too! For your information, there are plenty of white people in Cuba. Blonds even! My own mother is as light as you are!

ORQUIDEA: There are always accidents of nature.

CARLOTTA: (*Taking real offense.*) Then what kind of crash were you in! Your own daughter's not exactly Snow White, you know? I don't care what color make-up she wears.

SOLEDAD: Carlotta, please . . .

ORQUIDEA: If you spent more time outdoors, you'd have a sunburn, too.

CARLOTTA: Then you must have had her on the beach, because with her coloring, your womb must be sunburned!

ORQUIDEA: Carlotta!

CARLOTTA: No! Look at Ramonita! I dare any of you to tell me she's not white!

RAMONITA: Leave me out of this. (*However CARLOTTA has her by the arm and is dragging her towards* SOLEDAD.)

CARLOTTA: No! We'll see who's darker . . . The Cuban or the Puerto Rican!

SOLEDAD: Stop it, already!

RAMONITA: You're spilling my drink!

ORQUIDEA: Be careful with her dress! (*But* CARLOTTA *is determined and she puts their arms together,* RAMONITA *obviously is lighter.*)

CARLOTTA: There! You see? Case closed!

ORQUIDEA: It's just that her arms are like that! From wearing short sleeves!

CARLOTTA: Yeah? Well, then show me her behind!

SOLEDAD: Carlotta, enough! Please! Who gives a damn?

CARLOTTA: I do! *Carajo,* if I'm so black, Doña Orquídea, I think you'd be ashamed to have me be in your wedding.

ORQUIDEA: Nobody is forcing you to do it, you know? In fact, why don't you and Soledad spend the day together!

CARLOTTA: No, no. I want to do it. I want a picture of us together to send to the boys fighting in Africa!

SOLEDAD: Will you calm down, Carlotta? Don't let her get to you like this! You know how she is. My God, you should only hear what she says about my sister-in-law.

ORQUIDEA: Well, that one's not even Cuban. That one's just a no good tramp.

SOLEDAD: No she's not, Mama! She's a decent, hardworking

woman. You should only see how well she's bringing up her kids. And if you'd ever let her come here, you'd know it!

ORQUIDEA: *¡Una puta asquerosa es lo que es!*

SOLEDAD: How dare you go to church? How dare you take communion?

ORQUIDEA: How dare you even mention me and that woman in the same breath?

SOLEDAD: Why? Because she left her husband for a black man? Her alcoholic husband for a black man who's fighting right alongside our boys? Who may die, just like they might?

Tell me, Mama, didn't Don Felipe walk out on you? And you not only mention him, you're remarrying him! But he left you for a white woman, so I guess that makes everything different. That makes everything okay!

ORQUIDEA: You can't resist it, can you? You can't even let one day go by without having to drag that man's good name through the mud!

SOLEDAD: The only thing that man was good for was beating the hell out of me! In fact, he was a champion at it! You both were!

ORQUIDEA: That's what you said! That's what you told everybody! That's why he finally left! When we both know if he ever hit you it was for your own good! To take the defiance out of you the way you should be trying to take it out of that snot-nosed brat of a daughter of yours!

SOLEDAD: You leave Evelyn out of this!

ORQUIDEA: Well, if you're not careful she's going to end up just like you did! Fifteen and pregnant leaving you the embarrassment of forcing a boy to marry her!

TESSIE: (*Bursting into tears.*) Skippy! Oh God, I miss Skippy!

SOLEDAD: I never wanted you to do that! I never asked you to do that!

ORQUIDEA: What else could I do? Let you turn into a little whore?

SOLEDAD: I'd rather be one than be like you or Felipe, with your Bibles in one hand and your sticks in the other, trying to beat me into submission!

ORQUIDEA: We never beat you like that! Maybe if we had you'd have turned into a proper woman!

SOLEDAD: That's right, Mama, lie all you want! Stand there like the Madonna and lie! Just like you lie to Armando! Just like you'd lie to the neighbors! To the doctors! To the police whenever they would have to be called! Go ahead, Mama, lie! The way you'd make me lie for you, too! Make me tell people I fell down playing. That I had an accident in the street!

ORQUIDEA: You are drunk!

SOLEDAD: I am alive! That's what you really resent! You never buried the past, Mama. You buried yourself and you tried to bury me with you! Look at yourself, Mama. All dressed in black . . . In mourning for the world when all you're really mourning is your own suicide. That's the real reason you can't stand to see people having fun . . . The real reason you go to church . . . the real reason you even love this Goddamned war so much. It gives you something to do. A reason to be alive because you have no good reason of your own, you sanctimonious hypocrite! You're a dead woman, Mama. As dead as these damned statues Felipe sells from his pushcart on the street! (*She sends one crashing to the ground* ORQUIDEA *stands there stunned as do the rest of the women.*)

LILLIAN: So much for old times.

ORQUIDEA: (*After a pause.*) I'm just glad all of your friends are here to see for themselves how you really feel about me. To see for themselves what kind of a daughter you really are! But I warn you, this isn't over yet. You will be paid back for this! As surely as Judas betrayed Christ and Lucifer, God, so shall God Almighty betray you! So shall you be cast into hell for what you've done to me, to kiss the Devil forever!

SOLEDAD: I'm still living with you, Mama. How much more damned can I possibly be? (*The two women stand facing each other, their eyes locked in combat.*)

TESSIE: (*After a pause.*) Does this mean the party's over? (*Black out. As the house lights come up we hear the Andrews Sisters singing "Yes, My Darling Daughter."*)

ACT TWO

SCENE ONE

In the darkness the song, "Se Form ó El Bochinche" is heard.

We are back in the factory, Monday morning, where RAMONITA, CARLOTTA *and* TESSIE *are huddled together, gossiping amongst themselves. As the music fades the door opens and they each quickly take their places; however, it is* LILLIAN *who enters, a bit off center, as if her weekend has continued into this morning.*

TESSIE: Well, where were you all night?

LILLIAN: Don't you ever get tired of asking stupid questions?

RAMONITA: You're always so charming in the morning, Lillie.

LILLIAN: Oh, please, I had enough of you the other night. So where's the Orchid? She's usually in full bloom by now.

TESSIE: Nobody knows where she is.

LILLIAN: Maybe there is a God.

TESSIE: Soledad hasn't shown up either.

CARLOTTA: They're not coming in today. I tell you, they're not coming in.

LILLIAN: They'll be here.

CARLOTTA: What do you wanna bet?

LILLIAN: Nothing. I don't want to take your money.

CARLOTTA: Oh, sure. Sure.

LILLIAN: Okay, how much?

CARLOTTA: Ten cents.

LILLIAN: For ten cents I don't bother.

CARLOTTA: Because you know I'll win.

LILLIAN: Yeah? Well, you're on.

CARLOTTA: Wait a minute, you know something, don't you? You know what happened. You were with Soledad last night, right?

LILLIAN: The last I saw Soledad was at the Palladium Saturday night, just like the rest of you. But believe me, she'll be here. They both will. It will surprise me more if they're not.

TESSIE: Well, I was sure surprised to see Soledad go at Doña Orquídea like that. And then to turn around and walk out on her?

RAMONITA: It's about time somebody told her where to get off. If I didn't need this lousy job so much, I'd have done it myself a long time ago. Well, it's my own fault. Ralfie warned me not to take it.

LILLIAN: Already with Ralfie.

TESSIE: I don't care what anybody says, Doña Orquídea has every right to be hurt. Soledad really should be helping her with her wedding.

RAMONITA: Of course you'd side with Orquídea. After all, you're her little pet.

TESSIE: What's the matter? Are you jealous she didn't ask you to be her matron of honor?

CARLOTTA: I just wish I knew where Soledad went. I mean one minute she seemed to be having such a great time and the next minute she was gone, without so much as saying good-bye. Where the heck can she be?

LILLIAN: Since you're that interested, why don't you ask your spirits about it?

CARLOTTA: I did. But they told me to mind my own business. Just like I'm telling you.

TESSIE: I bet she's found herself a big palooka, that's what

I bet.

LILLIAN: Some people shouldn't be allowed to go to the movies.

CARLOTTA: I don't know. If I were her, that's what I would have done.

LILLIAN: Oh, please. We all know you prefer the company of your finger. At least when you can't find a pl tano around.

CARLOTTA: That was low, Lillie. Even for you.

TESSIE: What's wrong with *plátanos?* I love fried bananas.

CARLOTTA: She wasn't talking about frying them. At least not on the stove. TESSIE: What else are you gonna do with a big raw banana like that? (*The women look at her a moment causing her to think.*) Oh, my God, I'll never touch one of those things again! Who knows where it might have been?

LILLIAN: Like they say, necessity is the mother of invention.

TESSIE: Speaking of necessities, I've got to go back to the dentist today. My tooth is acting up again.

RAMONITA: I thought you had it taken care of Friday.

TESSIE: I did, but the filling fell out.

LILLIAN: Sounds like Manolo.

TESSIE: In a way I hope Doña Orquídea doesn't show up today. That way I can just leave and not have to ask her permission.

CARLOTTA: What are you worried about? When has she ever said no to you? Sometimes I think she wishes you were her daughter instead of Soledad.

TESSIE: Maybe because I respect her. Something none of you seem to do.

RAMONITA: I just hope Soledad is all right. It's not like her to disappear like this.

LILLIAN: Maybe she's with Ralfie?

RAMONITA: Oh, shut up, Lillie. I have a feeling she didn't go home all weekend. I tried calling her all day yesterday and she wasn't there.

TESSIE: I know. Doña Orquídea called me last night. The poor woman sounded so lonely I invited her over for dinner.

LILLIAN: Remind me to fumigate the place. You know, Tessie, people are gonna start talking about you two.

TESSIE: Oh, melon balls.

CARLOTTA: No. Soledad got home and she and Orquídea killed each other. That's what happened. I'm sure of it. (*Suddenly the door opens and* ORQUIDEA *enters, looking as if she hasn't slept.*)

LILLIAN: Yeah? Well, speak of the dead, look what just walked in. (*Relishing ORQUIDEA's condition.*) Good morning, Doña Orquídea.

ORQUIDEA: (*Her voice raspy.*) Good morning. (*She moves to her table and begins trying to work. The women continue to gossip amongst themselves.*)

LILLIAN: (*Quietly to the others.*) Get a load of beauty. She looks worse than I do Monday mornings.

TESSIE: Nobody looks worse than you do Monday mornings.

LILLIAN: You're not exactly too pretty with your head in the toilet bowl throwing up your guts every morning either.

TESSIE: You're such a blabbermouth, you know that? My tooth hurts. You know I can't stand pain.

CARLOTTA: I don't know about the rest of you, but I'm worried about her. She looks terrible. Do you think maybe Felipe ran out on her again?

RAMONITA: You're just hoping you won't have to wear that dress.

TESSIE: Maybe something did happen to Soledad. It's possible. Jeepers, it's more than possible. Oh my God, Lillie, talk to Doña Orquídea. Ask her about Soledad.

LILLIAN: I look like Charlie McCarthy to you? Do your own talking.

TESSIE: Oh, come on, please? Pretty please with sugar on it? I'll never tell you you're fat again.

LILLIAN: Listen, I'm not your mother, all right? From now on if you wanna know something, find out yourself. I'm tired of answering all of your stupid questions.

TESSIE: Well, if you feel that way about it, then okey dokey, I will. (*She pauses a moment, building up her courage.*) Doña Orquídea?

ORQUIDEA: (*Gruffly.*) What is it?

TESSIE: I was just wondering if you . . . if you . . . (*She halts, terrified.*)

ORQUIDEA: If I what?

TESSIE: If you would mind letting me leave a little early again today. I've got to go back to the dentist.

LILLIAN: (*Under her breath.*) Idiot. (*To* ORQUIDEA.) What she really wants to know, Doña Orquídea, is where is Soledad this morning?

ORQUIDEA: Don't you have any work to do?

LILLIAN: I am working, see? (*She runs a piece through the machine.*)

ORQUIDEA: With your mouth, maybe. And that goes for all the rest of you. Yakety, yakety, yak! Day in and day out! The same nonsense.

CARLOTTA: We were just worried about her, that's all.

ORQUIDEA: You want to know about Soledad? Ask your crystal ball.

CARLOTTA: I don't have a crystal ball.

ORQUIDEA: Then buy one!

CARLOTTA: (*Whispering to the girls.*) You see? We were right. She never went home.

ORQUIDEA: I'm sure you all know perfectly well where she is.

RAMONITA: We don't, honestly.

ORQUIDEA: Since when have you ever been honest with me? Since when have any of you ever been honest with me? No, Doña Orquídea is just here to let you leave early and come in late. To cover up for your mistakes. Well, no more. I cover up for nobody! I am tired of always being nice to you women. My God, I even asked you to be in my wedding party and still what do I get for it? All of you laughing at me behind my back, that's what I get! Like I don't know English. Like I'm deaf or something. Well, let me tell you, I hear everything you say. I see everything you do!

CARLOTTA: Maybe it's you who should be the spiritualist.

ORQUIDEA: I don't need witchcraft to tell me what to do and what not to do! It's God who walks with me. It's Him who tells me how to live my life!

LILLIAN: Well, the next time you're walking with Him, would you mind asking where Ralfie is? Ramonita's getting on my nerves talking about him all the time. (RAMONITA *is about to answer her; however, their attention is diverted to* SOLEDAD *who enters, now blonde and dressed to the hilt, in an ensemble that resembles something Marlene Dietrich would wear.*)

TESSIE: Jumping butterballs! (ORQUIDEA, *too, is speechless a moment, then turns back to the others.*)

ORQUIDEA: Get to work, all of you! (*The women resume their work, keeping an eye on* SOLEDAD *as she ambles over to her machine, making somewhat of a display of her unconcern with* ORQUIDEA.)

RAMONITA: (*Whispering.*) You look sensational. Absolutely sensational!

TESSIE: Jeepers, you're a regular pin up!

LILLIAN: Come on, Carlotta. Fork up your dime. I told you she'd be here.

CARLOTTA: Oh, no. You said Soledad would be here. You didn't say anything about Marlene Dietrich.

SOLEDAD: You took bets on me?

TESSIE: Only Carlotta and Lillie.

SOLEDAD: Thanks. Makes me feel like I should be running in the Kentucky Derby.

LILLIAN: Come on, pay up.

CARLOTTA: (*Giving her the dime.*) This is one bet I don't mind losing. The way you walked in was better than a movie. A double feature!

RAMONITA: I don't believe you actually went out and did it.

SOLEDAD: Does it look that terrible?

RAMONITA: No, it looks great. I'm just shocked, that's all.

LILLIAN: Even I'm impressed.

SOLEDAD: I don't know. I think I hate it.

TESSIE: Take it from me. You're a real fashion plate.

SOLEDAD: Now I know I hate it.

LILLIAN: So, where have you been?

SOLEDAD: What makes you think I've been anywhere?

LILLIAN: Look in the mirror and ask me that again.

CARLOTTA: Come on, Soledad, I'm dying to know. Where did you go after you left the Palladium?

SOLEDAD: (*For* ORQUIDEA's *benefit.*) Heaven. At least that's what they called the motel. God, I could have stayed in that room forever. I don't remember a bed ever feeling so good. I tell you, I must have run room service ragged. I don't think I'll ever cook for myself again. (ORQUIDEA *is doing her best not to show any response.*)

LILLIAN: Well, you were sure cooking on the dance floor. That guy who called himself Rubberlegs wouldn't leave me alone after you left. He kept hounding me for your number.

SOLEDAD: (*Again a little too loud.*) Really? How nice. (*Then in a whisper.*) I hope you didn't give it to him.

LILLIAN: No, but he pestered me so much about it, I ended up giving him mine.

RAMONITA: You would.

LILLIAN: (*Indicating* RAMONITA.) On the subject of pests, did anybody get a load of this number? After a couple of drinks any guy who asked her to dance was starting to remind her of Ralfie.

RAMONITA: That's not true.

LILLIAN: What's the matter, you have a blackout? You kept cornering everybody going . . . (*Imitating her.*) "Doesn't he look just like Ralfie? Doesn't he smile just like Ralfie? Doesn't he dance just life Ralfie?" God, I was waiting for

199

one of them to fart so you could say, "Doesn't he smell just like Ralfie?"

RAMONITA: You don't know what you're talking about.

LILLIAN: I just hope they hurry up and find him so I don't have to hear about him anymore. I was never that fond of him to begin with.

RAMONITA: Why? Because he was the one guy who wouldn't sleep with you?

LILLIAN: Sweetheart, I had him and threw him back. I want a man in bed, not a poet.

SOLEDAD: Come on, Lillie, don't say that.

RAMONITA: Let her talk. Cows have to do something with their own mouths when they're not grazing.

LILLIAN: Keep it up, toots, and your teeth are gonna be missing in action.

ORQUIDEA: (*Rechanneling her anger.*) That's enough from the both of you! Must you women talk non-stop? Can't you be silent for five minutes?

CARLOTTA: (*To* RAMONITA.) Watch it with Lillian today. I have the feeling she's already had a few.

RAMONITA: So what else is new? (*She works for a moment then turns back to* LILLIAN.) I'd like to see how you'd feel if it was Manolo who was missing?

LILLIAN: If Manolo was missing I'd give a party and invite any man who could walk.

RAMONITA: Why not? That's what you do anyway.

LILLIAN: At least I'm not frustrated, honey. And I don't need to hide behind bullshit commie politics to cover it!

RAMONITA: I know damned well what you need, Lillie! Only I'm too much of a lady to say it.

LILLIAN: You bitch! If you were any kind of lady. Any kind of a woman, instead of going to all your stupid meetings, at least for your Ralfie's sake, you'd be supporting your country. You'd be supporting the war.

RAMONITA: It's for Ralfie's sake that I don't! As much as your goddamned Roosevelt would have you believe different.

ORQUIDEA: I said that is enough! I will not have you talk about Roosevelt like that. He is a great man! A great leader!

RAMONITA: Leading a lot of young boys to their deaths is all he's doing!

ORQUIDEA: Sometimes there is greatness in death! Honor in giving your life for what you believe in!

RAMONITA: I'm sorry, Doña Orquídea, but I want more than a flag to take to bed with me at night. I want my husband!

ORQUIDEA: Sometimes a flag is all you get.

LILLIAN: Or whoever else happens to be around.

RAMONITA: Why don't you shut your fat drunken mouth already!

LILLIAN: Why don't you make me? (RAMONITA *jumps on her and they fight.*)

ORQUIDEA: Stop it! Enough! The both of you! I said stop it! (*The others manage to separate them.*)

RAMONITA: Doña Orquídea . . .

ORQUIDEA: The next one who says a word is fired! (RAMONITA *continues to stare angrily at* LILLIAN, *then they both resume work.*)

SOLEDAD: (*To* LILLIAN.) Next Christmas I'm gonna buy the both of you boxing gloves, the way you've been going at each other.

LILLIAN: You weren't exactly quiet the other night with your mother, but I suppose it's all right for you to get angry. The rest of us are always just supposed to keep it inside, right?

SOLEDAD: I'm sorry. I didn't mean anything by it. Hey, are you okay?

LILLIAN: Don't worry your little blonde head about it. (*After a moment they silently go back to work.* TESSIE *who has been watching* SOLEDAD, *suddenly moves to her.*)

TESSIE: I can't stand it anymore. You have to tell me where you got your hair done. You just have to.

SOLEDAD: I did it myself.

TESSIE: Really? Would you do mine? Oh, please? I bet I'd look just like Eva Perón.

SOLEDAD: I don't know.

TESSIE: Oh, please, please, please, please? I'd give anything to have my hair look like that for the wedding. Anything.

SOLEDAD: You like it so much? Here! it's yours! (*She takes it off and we see that it was only a wig which she angrily slaps down on* TESSIE's *head.*)

CARLOTTA: I knew it was a wig.

SOLEDAD: Oh, no, you didn't.

CARLOTTA: Oh, yes, I did. I have a doll who's got one just like it.

ORQUIDEA: (*Who has been keeping a constant eye on* SOLEDAD *moves to her.*) Soledad . . . (SOLEDAD *pays her no attention.*) Soledad . . .

SOLEDAD: (*To the others.*) Did you hear something? (*The others continue working, not wanting to get involved.*)

ORQUIDEA: (*Stronger this time.*) Soledad!

SOLEDAD: (*Snapping at her.*) Señora Ramírez to you! (OR-QUIDEA *pauses a moment, regaining her composure.*)

ORQUIDEA: We have to talk.

SOLEDAD: Is it about work?

ORQUIDEA: No.

SOLEDAD: Then I'm sorry, Doña Orquídea, but I'm very busy.

ORQUIDEA: That can wait.

SOLEDAD: So can you. Now if you'll excuse me? (OR-QUIDEA *watches her a moment as* SOLEDAD *continues sewing.*)

ORQUIDEA: Very well, Señora Ramírez, enjoy your silence. As I will mine. (*She goes back to her table and her work.*)

TESSIE: (*After a pause.*) You know, Soledad, you really shouldn't be that way with your mother.

SOLEDAD: This doesn't concern you, Tessie.

TESSIE: You know how you are with your daughter. How'd you like it if Evelyn . . .

SOLEDAD: I said to mind your own business, will you? (*After a moment she turns to* LILLIAN.) I don't know how you can put up with that girl sometimes.

LILLIAN: You're just finding out? God, I feel like going home tonight and getting so drunk, I disgust even myself.

SOLEDAD: Why don't we get drunk together? In fact, ladies, why don't we finish the party we tried to have the other day?

RAMONITA: I don't really feel like a party.

LILLIAN: Me neither.

SOLEDAD: Oh, come on. Doña Orquídea has choir practice tonight. We can have a good time without having anybody sitting there in judgement on us.

LILLIAN: Tonight I think I'm best off being alone.

CARLOTTA: Well, not me. I'm alone too much as it is. I'll bring up something to munch on.

SOLEDAD: Ramonita? Lillie?

LILLIAN: (*Giving in.*) Okay. Okay, but I have to stop home first. These clothes are starting to stick to me. I've been in them since yesterday.

SOLEDAD: And bring over any extra liquor you've got. Let's really tie one on.

TESSIE: Soledad?

SOLEDAD: What is it now, Tessie?

TESSIE: Am I invited, too?

SOLEDAD: Of course you're invited, Tessie.

TESSIE: Good. I'll stop by after the dentist. Only I can't bring anything. I'm on a tight budget.

RAMONITA: If he's under ninety, bring your dentist . . . for Lillie.

LILLIAN: Listen, if I hear one more crack out of you . . .

SOLEDAD: Leave it alone, Lillie.

LILLIAN: What are you taking her side for? She's the one who started it.

SOLEDAD: I'm not taking anybody's side. What's the matter with you today, Lillie?

LILLIAN: Nothing. Absolutely nothing. (*After a pause she turns to* SOLEDAD *and says quietly, so no one else can hear.*) Manolo's coming home. He's being given a Section Eight.

SOLEDAD: What?

LILLIAN: It seems he went off again. They found him drunk in a whorehouse beating up one of the girls. It took four M.P.'s to get him off of her. They should have just shot the son of a bitch.

SOLEDAD: I'm sorry, Lillie.

LILLIAN: Well, that's it, I guess. The war is over for me. And my side's lost. Fuck it! I should be used to losing by now. (*She turns back to her work. The women continue sewing as the lights dim. Blackout. In the darkness Xavier Cugat's version of "Siboney" begins.*)

ACT TWO

SCENE TWO

The lights come up DSL on LILLIAN's *apartment as* CARLOTTA *paces back and forth, listening to the music on the phonograph. She finishes up her drink, and though not her first, she still is in control.*

CARLOTTA: (*Calling offstage.*) Come on, Lillie. How long does it take you to get dressed?

LILLIAN: (*Offstage.*) I'll be right out. Make yourself another drink.

CARLOTTA: Please, I'm already pie-eyed as it is. Besides, there's going to be nothing left for the others.

LILLIAN: (*Offstage.*) So we'll stop and buy another bottle on the way. (*She enters, visibly intoxicated, in a sexy, low cut, suggestive outfit, holding up her empty glass.*) What do you think?

CARLOTTA: (*A bit taken aback.*) I think we'd better go.

LILLIAN: What's the rush? Anyway, I thought you said you wanted to talk to me. That is why you came home with me, isn't it? Well, talk.

CARLOTTA: Okay, Lillie. I really don't like the way you've been treating Ramonita. I want you to stop.

LILLIAN: In case you haven't noticed, Ramonita's a big girl. She doesn't need you to protect her.

CARLOTTA: She's my niece and I love her. I don't like to see her hurt. Ever since Ralfie disappeared you haven't exactly been too understanding. In fact, you've been a downright bitch, when what you should be is thanking God it's not your own husband who's missing.

LILLIAN: It should be! It should be Manolo who's missing. And if God was a woman he would be.

CARLOTTA: (*After a pause.*) I think maybe I will have that drink.

LILLIAN: (*Another pause as she starts to make the drinks.*) Believe it or not, Carlotta, I'm glad you're here. Even if it is only to tell me off. Still, anything's better than talking to Tessie lately. She's really starting to drive me crazy, you know?

CARLOTTA: Yeah, I know. She can be a little strange.

LILLIAN: Strange? If the rest of Argentina is like her, no wonder they're not in the war.

CARLOTTA: I'm surprised you two became friends in the first place.

LILLIAN: I needed help with the rent and she needed a place to live, what with apartments so scarce. Her own place reminded her too much of old Skippy boy. Still, sometimes I'd like to send her back to Argentina . . . via my foot. Hey, maybe we should send her over to Ramonita's and you and I should live together.

CARLOTTA: Are you kidding? We'd kill each other. Besides, I like things fine just the way they are.

LILLIAN: Sure you do.

CARLOTTA: What's that supposed to mean?

LILLIAN: Nothing. Why does everything always have to mean something?

CARLOTTA: Because it usually does.

LILLIAN: Not to me. In fact, most things mean nothing.

CARLOTTA: I think you've had one too many, Lillie. You're starting to talk stupid.

LILLIAN: Say a prayer for me then.

CARLOTTA: I pray for all of my friends.

LILLIAN: I am your friend, you know . . . I pray too, sometimes. Except I pray the war never ends. That it goes on forever.

CARLOTTA: I think you should have some coffee.

LILLIAN: Once it's over everything will go back to being just like it was before, only Manolo will be back and be even crazier than he was before he left . . . I pray that he dies.

CARLOTTA: For the love of God, don't say that. Look, instead of going over to Soledad's why don't you go inside and lie down for a while?

LILLIAN: Why don't you come inside and lie down with me?

CARLOTTA: (*Pauses, not sure if she's heard right.*) What was that?

LILLIAN: Oh, quit playing games.

CARLOTTA: You're the only one playing games here.

LILLIAN: What are you so afraid of?

CARLOTTA: I'm not afraid of anything. I just don't like the conversation.

LILLIAN: The conversation, or me?

CARLOTTA: One of these days that mouth of yours is going to get you into real trouble. I don't wonder why Manolo used to hit you.

LILLIAN: He didn't hit me because of anything I said! He hit me because he's a damned sadist, that's why he hit me! He enjoys hitting women. Probably because he can't do anything to them in bed.

CARLOTTA: If he's that terrible, why do you stay with him? Why don't you just leave him?

LILLIAN: Maybe I like getting beat up? Don't you think I tried? The bastard almost killed me. On my fucking honeymoon he knocked every tooth in my damned mouth out! Not to mention what he did to the rest of my body! Well, at least it took care of bringing any more little Manolo's into the world. No, Carlotta, I don't think I'll ever try to leave him again.

CARLOTTA: Look, let me make you some coffee. You'll feel better.

LILLIAN: I told you I don't want any coffee. What I want right now is you.

CARLOTTA: Why are you doing this to me, Lillie? Why me? Why now?

LILLIAN: Because right now I need somebody and I know you won't hurt me. No woman can possibly hurt another as much as a man takes a pleasure in. Our amusement lies elsewhere. Or don't you understand that?

CARLOTTA: All I understand right now is that you're a little drunk and a lot lonely.

LILLIAN: And aren't you?

CARLOTTA: Listen, I'm not a dog that goes around screwing whatever I can! When I go to bed with somebody I hope it's because we both want to. Not just because we need to.

LILLIAN: What are you getting so upset about? What am I doing except offering you a little bit of love.

CARLOTTA: Well, offer it to me tomorrow when you're sober. I don't like taking advantage of people. The same way I don't like people taking advantage of me. How did you even know about me?

LILLIAN: You don't need a Tarot card to figure out everything. For one thing you're too happily unmarried.

CARLOTTA: Is it that obvious, or did somebody tell you something? Somebody told you something, right?

LILLIAN: Nobody had to tell me anything. Believe me, Carlotta, I know you. Maybe even better than you know yourself. (TESSIE *enters in a fury and stands facing* LILLIAN, *about to explode.*) What the hell are you looking at me like that for? Hey, what's the matter? Fred and Ginger die?

TESSIE: No, Fred and Ginger didn't die. But the rabbit did!

LILLIAN: My condolences to your dentist.

TESSIE: I wasn't at my dentist! Oh God, I hate you, Lillie. With all of my heart, I hate you!

LILLIAN: What did I ever do to you?

TESSIE: I'm pregnant, that's what you did!

CARLOTTA: Oh, shit.

LILLIAN: So what are you blaming me for?

TESSIE: Because it's your fault!

CARLOTTA: Try to calm down, Tessie.

TESSIE: That's easy for you to say. You're not the one with a bun in the oven!

LILLIAN: So who's the proud father? Or don't you know?

TESSIE: Of course I know. It's Joe Joe. At least I think it's him.

LILLIAN: You think? You mean you're not sure?

TESSIE: I'm sure, I'm sure! But it only happened once!

CARLOTTA: Once is all it takes. Have you told him yet?

TESSIE: I just came from his house, but all he did was laugh and wish me a happy Mother's Day.

LILLIAN: And you, idiot, didn't even get a pair of stockings.

TESSIE: I didn't do it for a pair of stockings! I did it because he put something in my drink he said would make me feel good . . . Would make me forget all about Skippy.

CARLOTTA: So what are you blaming Lillian for?

TESSIE: Because she's the one who told me if he wore boots while he was doing it, this kind of thing could never happen.

CARLOTTA: Boots?

LILLIAN: I said rubbers, you idiot, not boots!

TESSIE: Boots! Rubbers! They're both the same thing!

LILLIAN: In Argentina maybe! Here, boots you put on your

feet. Rubbers he puts on his thing!

TESSIE: What thing?

LILLIAN: His pee pee, you idiot! His prick!

TESSIE: Now you tell me!

LILLIAN: God, how stupid can you be?

TESSIE: Don't yell at me! How was I supposed to know? Skippy's the only other man I've ever been with and he never even wore socks! He wanted to have a baby!

CARLOTTA: And I thought I had problems.

TESSIE: Oh God, what are people gonna say? What's Doña Orquídea gonna say? What's everybody gonna say?

LILLIAN: Why does anybody even have to know about it? You can always just get rid of it if you want.

TESSIE: And just how do you propose I do that?

LILLIAN: I don't know. Use a pencil. Flush it down the toilet, for all I care. Just leave me alone about it.

TESSIE: I wish it was you I could flush down the toilet! I hate you, Lillian! I hate you! I wish I could kill you and then kill myself!

LILLIAN: Go ahead. You'd be doing me a favor!

CARLOTTA: Will the both of you just stop this! Isn't there enough killing going on in the world to satisfy everybody? Doesn't anybody in this damned world want to live any-more? Well, you two go ahead and kill each other if you want. As for me, I'm going over to Soledad's. At least to her, life means something. (*She exits.*)

LILLIAN: (*Shouting after her.*) Wait a minute! You forgot the bottle! (*But* CARLOTTA *is gone. Then quietly after a pause.*) She forgot the bottle.

TESSIE: Why don't you go and bring it to her? And I hope you get hit by a car on the way.

LILLIAN: You know, Tessie, I'm glad Joe Joe laughed at you. I hope everybody laughs at you. At least maybe now you'll finally grow up. (*She exits with the bottle.* TESSIE *stands there not knowing what to do as the lights dim. Blackout. In the darkness the song "Cuando vuelva a tu lado" [What a Difference a Day Made] begins.)*

ACT TWO

SCENE THREE

The music continues as the lights rise, CS, on SOLEDAD's *apartment later that evening.* SOLEDAD, CARLOTTA, RAMONITA *and* LILLIAN *are playing cards, and though they've all had something to drink,* LILLIAN *is the only one who is feeling no pain, or rather every pain.*

LILLIAN: You sure know how to give a party, kiddo. Just warn me if there's gonna be another floorshow so I know when to duck.

SOLEDAD: There's gonna be one if a minute if you don't stop complaining. (*She listens to the music a moment.*) I used to love this song. Now all it is to me is a momento of the war. My first battle scar. Well, I guess every war has its music and this is my souvenir of this one.

CARLOTTA: What are you talking about? Does anybody know what she's talking about?

SOLEDAD: They were playing this the night before Armando left. He had taken me out to dinner and afterwards we went dancing. There was a girl singer. I don't remember her name. But anyway, she started singing this and I don't know. Armando and I seemed closer than we had been the whole time we'd been married. Then he told me my mother was moving back in with me and it was as if suddenly the whole world stopped. I couldn't hear anything but the music. Not even my own voice screaming he was a bastard and that I hated him. Needless to say we were asked to leave.

RAMONITA: Remind me never to invite you to any of my

going away parties.

SOLEDAD: I've never seen Armando look so frightened. He'd never seen me like that before. But he made a joke about it, like he does about everything else. He said when I yelled it made me look like my mother and if I wasn't careful, my face would freeze like that. God, that had to be the worst day of my life. Probably even worse than my wedding.

LILLIAN: Nothing was worse than your wedding. I've been to cemeteries with more life than that.

RAMONITA: What are you talking about? Doña Orquídea really went all out.

LILLIAN: Yeah. Crackers and cheese and one bottle of the cheapest champagne on the market.

CARLOTTA: You've got to be kidding? Was that really all she could afford?

SOLEDAD: It wasn't all she could afford, Carlotta. To her, it was more than I deserved. I was humiliated with Armando's family. At least the two of them that bothered to show up.

LILLIAN: Had I known what to expect, I wouldn't have shown up either . . . Hell with giving you a gift.

SOLEDAD: Still Armando didn't seem to mind even that. Even that he managed to find kind of funny. Then again he always did have a sick sense of humor.

LILLIAN: (*Bursting into laughter.*) He's not the only one! Remember that time we sent those love letters to Mother Superior signed Father Joseph? I think that's the first time she ever saw the word fuck written down in her life!

SOLEDAD: Oh, God, don't remind me . . .

RAMONITA: Or that time we locked Sister Aggie in the closet not to take that history test?

SOLEDAD: Please, my mother went crazy when she found out. Made me walk to and from church on my hands and knees every day for a month! I didn't think my knees would ever stop bleeding.

LILLIAN: My favorite was when we painted genitals on all the statues in the chapel.

RAMONITA: Boy, we really got it for that one. Worse than that Easter you got us to paint all the faces on Don Felipe's statues black!

SOLEDAD: Me?

RAMONITA & LILLIAN: You! (*They all laugh loudly as they remember.*)

CARLOTTA: No wonder they called you "The Terrible Trio." You were.

RAMONITA: I can't believe how much I still miss those times though. Even if we did always get caught. "The Terrible Trio." The only three Spanish girls in the school.

SOLEDAD: I know. It's hard to believe we were ever that young.

LILLIAN: And that stupid.

SOLEDAD: Not stupid, Lillie. Innocent.

LILLIAN: (*Suddenly angry.*) Then fuck innocence! Fuck it! The way it's fucked us! Innocence . . . (*She picks up the bottle.*) This is my innocence ladies. My innocence, my past and my future. All eighty proof of it!

CARLOTTA: Take it easy, Lillie.

LILLIAN: Don't tell me what to do, okay? Or okey dokey as the little mother would say. You had your chance.

SOLEDAD: I always thought when I got married everything would be different. That that's when everything would finally change. And here I am, just like the same stupid kid living under her mother's iron rule.

RAMONITA: Believe it or not, you are different now. We're all different. Maybe war does make a man out of boys like they say. But let me tell you, it sure as hell makes women out of little girls, too. Damned strong women.

SOLEDAD: Some woman I am. Look at yourself, Ramonita. How independent you are. How you always do whatever you want, even when everybody else is against it.

RAMONITA: Yeah. That's why I sit in the same factory, just like the rest of you . . . Sewing bits and pieces of blouses together, wishing the bits and pieces of my life fit together as easily. Believe me, Soledad, you're a lot smarter than you think. And a lot tougher.

SOLEDAD: Did you see me at the Palladium the other night? Sure I got up and danced and flirted and got flirted with, but to tell you the truth, inside all I felt was embarrassed. I was frightened and embarrassed and ashamed of myself, and not because I was doing anything wrong. It was just the first time in years I've gone anywhere without either my mother or my husband deciding where it should be. And I was frightened because I'd forgotten how good it felt. I was ashamed because I didn't want it to stop. It felt wonderful dancing whenever and with whomever I wanted. Having a drink without having to ask for approval. I don't remember the last time I was so happy just to be myself. Or the last time I felt so guilty because I wanted it to last forever.

RAMONITA: Why should you feel guilty? Believe me, we all feel that way sometimes, even if we don't admit it. Because you marry somebody shouldn't mean you have to give up who you are for them.

SOLEDAD: Tell that to Armando. Or didn't you see how much he changed?

RAMONITA: He grew up, that's all.

SOLEDAD: It's more than that. Remember how excited he used to be about life? That look of wildfire always in his eyes? God, it was like the electric lights were turned on whenever he entered the room.

LILLIAN: With Manolo it's just the opposite. He walks in and all the lights go out.

SOLEDAD: I wasn't even going to tell him I was pregnant, only my mother overheard me talking to you and Lillie and forget it. You think there's a war now?

CARLOTTA: Knowing her, I'm surprised she didn't just kill you.

SOLEDAD: That would have been too easy. Instead she went

charging over to his house, screaming that he had ruined my
life and now had to make up for it. And instead of even
trying to deny it, he just stood there and agreed. Just like he
agreed to have her move in with us to help out when I had
the baby. Then so he could finish school. Then when he
joined the service. Now it's the war. Just like he's agreed
with everything she's ever said! Even though I begged him
not to! But he believes her lies. He believes she's doing it
out of love for me!

LILLIAN: At least he loves you. God, I can't tell you how many
times I wished it had been me he had gotten pregnant.

SOLEDAD: Maybe he should have, Lillie. Maybe he'd be
happier with you. (ORQUIDEA *enters from the bedroom.*)

ORQUIDEA: I'll see you women later. Assuming you're still
here.

LILLIAN: Have a good time, Doña Orquídea. Sing one for me.

ORQUIDEA: Soledad?

SOLEDAD: Not now, Mama, please.

ORQUIDEA: I'll try not to be too late. I hope we can talk when
I get back.

SOLEDAD: (*Turning to her.*) Don't you understand I've got
nothing more to say to you? I don't even want to look at you
right now!

ORQUIDEA: Soledad . . .

SOLEDAD: Will you just hurry up and go already!

ORQUIDEA: Damn you, do you think nothing hurts me? That
I'm so devoid of feelings I can't be wounded?

SOLEDAD: I could slit your throat, Mama, and I don't think
you'd bleed.

ORQUIDEA: Yes, I bleed! Yes, I feel! Yes, I care! But no, not
you! You're the only one who feels anything! Who cares
about anything! Like you care so much about your husband!
Well, Señora Ramírez, you can stop your caring! (*Everything stops for a moment.*) While you were out all week-end,
Señora Ramírez, having yourself a grand old time, you had

a visitor. He left this for you. (*She takes out a telegram from her purse.* SOLEDAD *stands there a moment, not believing what is happening, as do the others who watch in silence.*) Here, take it, Señora Ramírez. It's addressed to you. (SOLEDAD *still cannot move.*) Take it! (*She flings the telegram at her and it lands on the floor.*)

LILLIAN: (*Softly.*) Oh, my God, no . . . (*After a moment* SOLEDAD *finds the strength to move and pick up the telegram, which she continues to look at in disbelief.*)

RAMONITA: I'm sorry, Soledad. I'm so sorry. (SOLEDAD *continues to stand there, then looks at* ORQUIDEA *helplessly.*)

SOLEDAD: Mama . . .

ORQUIDEA: I just thank God someone was here to answer the knock on the door. At least that's one humiliation God has spared me . . . Enjoy your party, ladies. (*She starts for the door.*)

CARLOTTA: How could you? How could you know about this all day and say nothing?

ORQUIDEA: It's she who wouldn't speak to me.

CARLOTTA: And you're really gonna go out now?

ORQUIDEA: I see no reason to stay. She's got her friends here for comfort. And if that's not enough she can always go back out and get it wherever she did this weekend.

CARLOTTA: That's terrific, Doña Orquídea, but I just remembered I have something to do next week-end, so don't expect me to be at your damned wedding.

ORQUIDEA: And you, Ramonita? Are you busy next Saturday as well? (RAMONITA *can only glare at her.*) Fine. And you can both use tomorrow to look for another job.

CARLOTTA: The hell with your job, Doña Orquídea, and the hell with you!

ORQUIDEA: Good night, ladies. My condolences to you, Señora Ramírez. (*She exits.*)

CARLOTTA: Jesus Fucking Christ! How did you ever survive her?

SOLEDAD: Have I? (*She quickly downs her drink.*) I tell you, if it wasn't for my own kid, I'd chalk it all up right now. Only I can't let her grow up like I did. She's gotta know that somebody loves her no matter what she does.

CARLOTTA: My mother loved me like that. Then she found out the truth about her little girl. Bought me a one way ticket to New York. Sometimes I wish she had never loved me at all.

SOLEDAD: I went up to see her yesterday. I planned to spend the whole day with her except all she did was complain that I'd forgotten to bring up the dress I made her. She kept saying I didn't love her. That I probably hadn't even made it. That the only one who loved her was her daddy and that her daddy was the only one she loved. I kept telling her to stop it but she wouldn't. She kept yelling at me. Yelling how much she loved her daddy and hated me. And suddenly it was like the night Armando told me my mother was moving back in. I found myself standing there unable to move. Unable to breathe. Unable to think. I didn't even realize I had begun hitting her. Hitting her with such a vengeance I was my mother all over again with her crying out for her daddy, the way I used to cry out for mine. God, how do I tell her now her daddy's not coming home? That all she has left is me! (*She rips open the telegram and stares at it a moment, sickened by the contents.*) Oh God . . . Oh God . . .

RAMONITA: I'm sorry, Soledad. (*However,* SOLEDAD*'s feelings soon turn to rage.*)

SOLEDAD: I'll kill her! I swear to God, I'll kill her!

CARLOTTA: What are you talking about? Soledad, what are you talking about?

RAMONITA: (*Reading the telegram.*) "Happy Anniversary, Love Orquídea."

CARLOTTA: Happy Anniversary, Love Orquídea? (*Suddenly an air raid siren blasts which is the last straw for* SOLEDAD.)

SOLEDAD: Goddamn you, Mama! No more! No more! No more! (*Blackout. In the darkness the first line of "Cuando Vuelva a Tu Lado" can be heard over and over again like on a record that is scratched.*)

ACT TWO

SCENE FOUR

The music continues a moment as the lights rise on SOLEDAD *sitting alone in her apartment later that night, the telegram in front of her. As the music fades, soft knocking on the door can be heard; however,* SOLEDAD *continues to sit there silently. The knocking comes again, then after a moment the door opens and* TESSIE *enters dressed in black, a sorrowful look on her face.*

TESSIE: (*After a pause.*) I'm sorry I couldn't get here sooner. (SOLEDAD *turns to her, surprised it is* TESSIE.) Lillie told me about the telegram. About Armando.

SOLEDAD: Armando? (*She almost laughs as* TESSIE *stands there pathetically.*) Take that look off your face, Tessie. Armando's not dead.

TESSIE: I know how you feel. I used to say that about Skippy, too.

SOLEDAD: I mean it, Tessie. Armando's as alive as I am. Probably more so.

TESSIE: But why would Lillie . . .?

SOLEDAD: You know Lillie. I'm sure it was just her idea of a joke.

TESSIE: A joke? That bitch! She knows I hate wearing black! I swear, I've had it with her. I've had it! Do you know what else she did to me today? Do you know what else she actually had the nerve to say to me today?

SOLEDAD: I don't want to hear about it right now, okay, Tessie?

TESSIE: She actually had the nerve to say . . .

SOLEDAD: Please, Tessie, not now!

TESSIE: Don't get angry at me. I haven't done anything to you.

SOLEDAD: It's not just you, Tessie. I'm angry at everything right now.

TESSIE: I'm angry, too. You know what Lillie . . .

SOLEDAD: Will you stop it with Lillie, already!

TESSIE: She's not your only friend, you know? Maybe I'm not part of the Terrible Trio, but I am your friend, too.

SOLEDAD: I don't think you know what being a friend really means, Tessie.

TESSIE: How can you say that to me? Is it because your mother likes me?

SOLEDAD: No, Tessie, because you're selfish . . . you're stupid. Because you live in a world that's totally unreal and expect the rest of us to do for you, while you give nothing in return. All you know how to do is take.

TESSIE: That's not true. That's really why I'm here. To give You something.

SOLEDAD: You've got nothing I want.

TESSIE: Don't do this to me, Soledad. At least hear me out. (*After a pause.*) Did Lillie tell you I'm pregnant?

SOLEDAD: Yes.

TESSIE: I want to have my baby, Soledad.

SOLEDAD: So have it.

TESSIE: How? Look at me. I can hardly take care of myself. I never even had a job before the war. I've always had someone to take care of me. How can I take care of a baby? But I can't kill it either. I thought maybe I could go away somewhere and have it and then I don't know . . . Maybe put it up for adoption.

SOLEDAD: Get to the point, Tessie.

TESSIE: I thought maybe I could give it to you. That you might be willing to take it.

SOLEDAD: Why would I want to do that?

TESSIE: You're good with kids, Soledad. And I am your friend, whether you believe it or not. And if you do take it then it's not like I would have to give it up altogether. I could still watch it grow up. I could still be a part of its life.

SOLEDAD: Without any of the responsibilities.

TESSIE: I'd pay you. I wouldn't ask you to do it for free. I would still work. I'd give you whatever money you needed to bring it up.

SOLEDAD: First off, Tessie, you're talking about a child, not an it. And a child needs love, not money to grow up. And I'm afraid right now I don't have any to spare. I've got enough problems of my own, without having to take on yours as well.

TESSIE: Then tell me what to do . . . please. (DOÑA OR-QUIDEA *enters from outside*.) Please, Soledad. (SOLEDAD *remains silently avoiding any contact with either her or* ORQUIDEA.)

ORQUIDEA: Tessie? Tessie, are you all right? Tessie? (TESSIE *looks up at her a moment, then exits quickly*.) What's the matter with Tessie? (SOLEDAD*'s only response is to light up a cigarette from a pack on the table*.) I see you've opened the telegram. Had you not stormed out of here like such a fury the other night, you would have gotten it on your anniversary like I planned. You'd know I had it sent with the best of intentions. You don't honestly think I would have left you alone if I thought something had happened to Armando?

SOLEDAD: I have no idea what you think. What goes on in that malicious mind of yours.

ORQUIDEA: Soledad . . .

SOLEDAD: I know you're a vindictive woman, Mama. That you've done despicable things out of anger . . . In your moments of rage, but to cold-bloodedly deliberately try to make me think my husband was dead . . . I had no idea anyone . . . even you could be so cruel.

ORQUIDEA: Whether you believe it or not, I did it for your own good.

SOLEDAD: My own good?

ORQUIDEA: I saw where you were heading, Soledad. How you were about to throw your life away again. Like you had done with Armando. And I wanted to prevent that. I wanted to show you how important it is for a woman to respect herself and her marriage at all costs. To hold on to her principles at all costs.

SOLEDAD: You have no principles, Mama! They're as phoney as your damned wedding is!

ORQUIDEA: Don't you dare say that to me! To hear you talk anyone would think I was the one guilty of abandoning my marriage. That I was the one out galavanting all over town this weekend betraying my husband.

SOLEDAD: I went to see my daughter, Mama. That's the adulteress I am.

ORQUIDEA: The whole time.

SOLEDAD: Yes, Mama, the whole time.

ORQUIDEA: I'm surprised you didn't go running to Victoria's. I'm sure she would have been more than happy to accommodate you.

SOLEDAD: Shut up, Mama. For once in your life just shut the hell up!

ORQUIDEA: (*She tries to slap her.*) I won't have you talk to me like this! (SOLEDAD *grabs her by the arm.*)

SOLEDAD: I'll talk to you anyway I want in my own house! And this is my house, Mama. My house!

ORQUIDEA: Really? Well, I wonder what Armando would say.

SOLEDAD: You write and you tell him whatever the hell you want, Mama, just so long as you write him from another address.

ORQUIDEA: What's that supposed to mean? Are you asking me to leave? Is that what you're doing?

SOLEDAD: I'm not asking you anything. I am throwing you

out! Something I should have done a long time ago! I want you as far away from me and my daughter as you can possibly get!

ORQUIDEA: Fine! Don't think it's been any great pleasure for me living here with you either. Believe me, I am more than happy to leave your house. I'm sure one of the ladies at the church will be willing to put me up for a week. God knows they've done it before when I've had nowhere else to go.

SOLEDAD: And about a week is all most of them could take of you.

ORQUIDEA: If not one of the ladies, I'll ask one of the priests. I can always make do on a cot in the church basement until next Saturday. I just thank God at least somebody in this world still takes pity on the destitute.

SSOLEDAD: Why not just move in with Don Felipe?

ORQUIDEA: Because unlike you, I have some respect for sanctity of marriage as well as for my body!

SOLEDAD: Good. Take your sanctity and go.

ORQUIDEA: You don't have to tell me again! I'm only surprised you haven't done this sooner. After all, it's what you've wanted all along. Now you're free to do as you please without having to worry about it. To make all the mistakes you want without having to worry about them. Without having to answer for them!

SOLEDAD: The only mistake I ever made was to get married, Mama! At least to Armando. I wanted to get pregnant. I planned it! For once in my life I wanted to have somebody whose love you couldn't deny me! Whose love you couldn't distort until you had made it as ugly as you had made mine! Why do you think I even made sure you found out about it?

ORQUIDEA: To hurt me! To humiliate me like you've always enjoyed doing!

SOLEDAD: I did it hoping to save my life! I knew exactly how you'd react. I knew you'd go running to Armando. And I knew he was too nice a guy not to marry me. It was the only way I could think of to finally escape from you! And I would have done anything to do that. Even trick a boy into marrying me! Only I never thought of the consequences. I never thought I'd be moving from one prison into another. Or that Armando would be weak enough to allow you to continue being a part of my life!

ORQUIDEA: You should thank God I've always been there to take care of you! To protect you!

SOLEDAD: You're the only one I've ever needed protection from! You couldn't care less about me, Mama. You've always just been afraid of being alone. Why the hell else do you think you're here! Certainly not out of any feelings for me! Well, I'm not afraid of it, Mama. I welcome it! In fact, the only thing I am afraid of is becoming any more like you than I already am!

ORQUIDEA: You could never be like me. Never!

SOLEDAD: I'm more like you than you know! You were right about me this weekend, Mama. I didn't just go to see Evelyn. I went out and found myself a man! An honest to God, red-blooded, one hundred per cent man! A man no woman could dominate! But even though I made him feel like it was the goddamned Fourth of July, just like you, Mama, I couldn't feel anything. No matter how much I wanted to. No matter how hard I tried. Just like you, Mama, I still couldn't feel anything. Just like you I am incapable of feeling. Incapable of loving. Incapable of knowing anything but rage!

ORQUIDEA: Right! I've never loved anybody! Never! I don't know what it is to be a woman. I've never needed anybody or anything! (*She pauses a moment as if not wanting to go on, then turns on* SOLEDAD *with full venom.*) You ignorant bastard! (*She is almost shaking with rage.*) When I met your father I loved that man more than God! Do you hear me? I wanted that man so much nothing else mattered to me but him! Not my family . . . my friends . . . my respectability . . .

nothing! Not even God Himself! And for all my love . . . for all that I gave him . . . there was less than nothing in return! No love. No wedding. No church. No money. Not even decency. And I didn't care! All I needed was him! Until one day he didn't need me anymore. Until one day he didn't want me anymore!

SOLEDAD: What? Then the death of Lieutenant Mallory is as much of a lie as the death of Armando?

ORQUIDEA: There is no Lieutenant Mallory! There never was a Lieutenant Mallory! Your father was no soldier . . . He was no hero . . . The only battles Jacinto Calderón ever fought were on the streets of Río Piedras with his whores! That's who your father was! Jacinto Calderón! A demon as black as the midnight sky with eyes that filled me with the flames of hell! Eyes I would look at while we danced naked in the shadow of the moon. Wild eyes. Crazy eyes. Eyes that made me long to fuck the devil. That is your father! And let me tell you, I worshipped every moment of it! I worshipped every moment of pain that was his paradise! I would get down on my knees and beg him for his desires. No matter how degrading. How depraved. I would get down on my knees and beg for more! I worshipped that man as I had once worshipped God Almighty! But even that wasn't enough for him. Not even my immortal soul was enough for him! And all I was left with was you inside me as a remembrance of my shame! That is the father you wanted to know. The man that I loved! A no good filthy bastard who left you inside me to disgrace my womb!

SOLEDAD: You maniac! You fanatic! You used me to atone your shame? You tortured me to repent your lust for a black man? For my father? Damn you, Mama! No matter who my father was . . . No matter how he treated you . . . I was born innocent! Innocent! Just like every other child ever born, I was born innocent! You had no right to hate me because of him! To try and destroy me because of him!

ORQUIDEA: I didn't hate you! I never hated you! Even though I'd pray to God everyday that I could! Maybe then I could hate him, too. Maybe then I could finally be free of him and the devil of me! All I ever wanted was for you to be the lady I should have been. The lady I was brought up to be. The lady I am!

SOLEDAD: Even if it killed me? You're no lady, Mama, I don't care how many hours a day you spend in church. (*She stands there a moment not knowing whether to laugh or cry.*) Damn you, Mama, didn't you know how much I loved you? How I would have done anything . . . Been anything you wanted had you only shown me the slightest affection? Even after you'd beat me, Mama, I'd tell myself it was my fault. That I was bad. That I had something evil in me. I believed you, Mama, I believed that's why God had even made my skin dark. To mark me for devil. I'd lie in bed at night, Mama, with my bones broken and my head split open and I'd pray, too. I'd pray when I woke up that by some miracle that evil would be gone. That by some miracle you would . . . you would . . . and then you married Don Felipe, Mama, and the only miracle I prayed for after that was that I'd survive. Goddamn you, Mama! All I ever wanted from you was love, and all you ever gave me was Ten Commandments bashed into my skull!

ORQUIDEA: Do you think I loved Don Felipe? Do you think I wanted to marry Don Felipe?

SOLEDAD: Then why did you, Mama? Why are you marrying him now?

ORQUIDEA: Because he's the only man who ever wanted to marry me! Don't you understand? Not just live with me . . . not just go to bed with me . . . Not just use me like your father had done . . . but marry me. He was the one man willing to give you his name and me back my honor.

SOLEDAD: Well, you can keep them both, Mama. I want no part of them.

ORQUIDEA: (*After a pause.*) I'm sorry, Soledad. I'm sorry.

SOLEDAD: So am I. It would have been nice to have a mother I didn't have to be afraid every time she touched me it would hurt. (*The two women remain there silently a moment.*)

ORQUIDEA: I'll send someone from the church to pick up my things. (*She hesitates a moment longer then starts for the door, but as she is about to open it she freezes. She speaks quietly without turning around; however, the panic in her voice is apparent.*) Please. Please, Soledad. Don't make me go out there alone now. I can't go to church. Don Felipe . . . not now. Not like this. (SOLEDAD *turns to her and the two women look at each other as if for the first time.*)

SOLEDAD: You have to go, Mama. And not because I hate you. In fact, despite what you've done to me, I think somewhere deep inside me I probably still even love you. But right now all I want . . . No, Mama, right now all I need is you out of my house and out of my life so that maybe . . . just maybe I can finally feel I have one of my own again that's worth living.

ORQUIDEA: God has already condemned me my soul! Please, please don't condemn me the rest of my life.

SOLEDAD: You've condemned yourself, lady, not me, by being unholy enough to have sentenced your daughter to a lifetime of pain. (ORQUIDEA *stands there a moment longer, then exits slowly.* SOLEDAD *stands there unmoving, then after a few moments goes and pours herself a drink. She takes a long sip and as she stands there her eyes go to the mirror. She walks slowly over to it and looks at her reflection a long moment. Softly.*) Damn you, Mama, I was innocent. I was innocent. (*She begins wiping away the mask of make-up off her face. The lights dim. Blackout. In the darkness "Rum and Coca-Cola" by the Andrews Sisters begins.*)